# AGAINST THE STREAM

*"Rex Hunt translates the academic word into the preached word. This is no easy task but he expertly reveals how the liberal Jesus is so much needed in contemporary society. In these wonderfully enlightening sermons we are transported across the centuries to the Jesus of history. We find, through Hunt's fine hermeneutical skills, the message of the teacher from Nazareth is still relevant and inspirational for people today"*

The Revd Canon Dr Nigel Leaves, Author of *Religion Under Attack*

Other Publications by Rex A. E. Hunt

(Collated and Edited)
*When We Come Together.*
*A Study of the Place and Practise of Worship and Liturgy*
(1984)

(Edited)
*New Green Shoots and Other Story Sermons*
(1993)

(Edited with John W. H. Smith)
*We Weren't Told!*
*A Handbook of 'progressive' Christianity*
(Forthcoming 2013)

# AGAINST THE STREAM

## PROGRESSIVE CHRISTIANITY BETWEEN PULPIT AND PEW

REX A.E. HUNT

MOSAIC PRESS

Mosaic Press
508 High St
Preston Vic. 3072
Australia

Mosaic Press is an imprint of Mosaic Resources Pty Ltd

ISBN 9781743240748



First published 2012

Cataloguing-in-Publication entry is available for the National Library of Australia http:/catalogue.nla.gov.au/.

Design by John Healy
Printed by Openbook Howden

“Sing praise to all that has opened our minds to new vistas—
All that has called us to seek out new truths through the ages:
Vision and word,
Music that sought to be heard
These are the gifts that will mould us”

*(Gretta Vosper, With or Without God)*

For
Dylis, with much love and gratitude

And thanks to the people of
The Church of St James, Canberra
(2000-2009)

# Contents

INTRODUCTION .......... 9

PREFACE

Progressive Christianity: From an Ancient Understanding of Faith into some New Possibilities.......... 15

REFLECTIONS

"Stay Alert! Advent 'Incarnation' from the Landscape".......... 35
"A Defiant Christmas as a Sign of Hope".......... 42
"Have Yourself a Very, Merry, 'Political' Christmas".......... 47
"Some Bells Jingle, and Some Bells Toll!".......... 55
"Celebration and the Presentness of God" .......... 60
"A 'Spirituality' on a Journey of Discernment".......... 64
"Snorting Indignation While Boundaries are Pushed" .......... 69
"Artisan Jesus and the Re-Imagined Kin-dom" .......... 74
"The Temptation to Do Good" .......... 79
"Truth... And Being a Blessing or a Curse" .......... 83
"The Palm Sunday Challenge to Set Jesus Free" .......... 89
"Good Friday: Not Being Defeated by Violence" .......... 93
"Life Invites Us To Be Startled By Easter, Not Scared By It".......... 97
"Transformations on the Edge of Time" .......... 102
"Pentecost: A Day to See 'Green' Amid the 'Red'! .......... 107
"Power Enabling, Rather than Power Over" .......... 113
"On Counting the Women and Children" .......... 119
"Fear and 'Stony Ground' in Times of Change" .......... 123
"A Ban on Divorce or a Ban on Legalism?" .......... 128
"Doers Rather than Caught in the Spell of Good Intentions Only".... 133

"Taxes Might Go to Caesar, but Thanks for the Pocket-money!"..... 138
"The 'Talent' of Being a Whistleblower"........................... 143
"At the Gates, Bearing the Passion of the Christ".................. 147
"Pluralism is Not Some Religious 'Fruit Salad"..................... 152
"The Earth that we Knew... is Gone. Long Live Eaarth!"........... 158
"Coming Home to the Cosmos"...................................... 165

AFTER WORD

"Against the Stream, While Continuing the Journey"............... 172

FURTHER READING.............................................. 182

ABOUT THE AUTHOR............................................ 184

# Introduction

I always saw myself as an enthusiastic student when I was in Theological College in the mid 1960s. But I was never content with the standard theological diet served up at the College.

Since those days I realise that some individual Faculty members in many such places are caught in a bind. Do they encourage their students to push boundaries outside the accepted 'texts' by 'challenging the tradition', or do they stay within—often following denominational requirements—'guarding the tradition' or "right understanding of the faith" *(Thompson 2011:17)*. Should anyone ever be in doubt, I have always come down in favour of the former rather than the latter!

So up front I want to express my gratitude to my Systematic Theology professor and Project supervisor, Dr Harry Wardlaw, for encouraging me to go on my own theological journey, more often than not, 'against the stream'.

As I have already alluded to, my personal progressive journey started during Theological College days. Having been given advice by my local minister that I should read the theology of a suspected 'heretic' called Samuel Angus, and been introduced to Process Theology by some student colleagues, a group of four of us, all then Presbyterians, agreed to establish an editorial committee and commence publication of an informal theological journal called: *Catalyst: A Journal of Progressive Religious Thought*. It had a small circulation, around 100 or so, and remained in publication for seven years until the end of 1974. This was probably the first time the term 'progressive' was intentionally used in relationship to Australian Christianity in particular.

Little remains of our printed efforts of progressive articles, sermons, reviews and liturgical offerings, as ink-soaked Gestetner stencils and high-acid duplicating paper were either destroyed or disintegrated—taking with them dreams as well as mistakes. Now there are progressive theology web sites worldwide! Prior to our publication the term generally used in such circles in Australia was 'liberal'. But as many of you would know, using that title is not always helpful in Australia, given its abuse by conservative 'right wing' politicians! So I am still very comfortable with the title 'progressive', and try to use it with a lower-case 'p' to indicate it is not another denomination or fixed category.

Often in those student days, as of now, I would go to a section in my personal library and pull out a copy of Henry Nelson Wieman's book, *The Wrestle Of Religion With Truth*.

I was first introduced to Wieman's thought by another student. Wieman's thought very quickly became part of my life. And despite several house-moves over the years since then, I have resisted the temptation to sell off his books because they are 'old' and now somewhat dated.

Wieman was a former professor in the Divinity School of the University of Chicago, USA, and this book, his second one, was published in 1928—which is a little before my time, I might add! In the opening chapter Wieman says:

> "With respect to religion there are three classes of people: the religious rationalizers, the irreligious rationalizers and the religiously inquisitive. The first class may think about religion from the outside to defend it; the second class may think about it from the outside to destroy it. But only the third class thinks about it from the inside with a view to discovering precisely what may be the good of it. It alone honestly inquires into its validity, its conditions and consequences..."
>
> *(Wieman 1928:35)*

Seeking to explain his comments a bit more, Wieman goes on to describe, in general terms, each class or group.

The first group, the "religious rationalizers", are generally very devout and earnest people. They acquired their religion in childhood or youth, or in some profound experience later in life, and it is a very precious thing. But it is complete and finished. They have nothing more to learn about it. They have only to enjoy it and use it.

All their religious discussions are not forms of inquiry but devises for stimulating further experiences. They want the experience and yearn for more and more of it and are eager to transmit it deeply and widely to others as self authenticating truths requiring uncritical assent. The ultimate worth and significance of their religion is never a matter of inquiry. Anything that has the hint of intellectual investigation about it and which is then applied to their religion, they bitterly resent.

The second group, the "irreligious rationalizers", also refuse to enter into any form of inquiry. Some of them studied it, in Sunday or boarding school, but it was presented in such a way they became sick and tired of it. For them it is a frightful bore, a foolish superstition, an evil influence.

They have no understanding of it. They have made up their minds they want nothing to do with it. They are unable to 'listen' and resent 'being forced' to give the matter any further consideration whatsoever.

On the other hand, the third group, the "religiously inquisitive", are intellectually alive. They do not think merely in order to defend. They think in order to understand. Wieman says:

> "Religion may be no less precious to them than to the first group, but for them the most precious things are subjects for investigation"
>
> *(Wieman 1928:37).*

Again—and please excuse the non-inclusive language:

> "... the first class, the devout and unthinking, have been the happiest, strongest and most effective of religious folk... For as soon as a man begins to think about anything, it begins to change for him.
> It takes on diverse shapes and hues. It swims about like a fish in the sea. Only if he refuses to think about his religion... can it remain unchanged like sardines in a can.
>
> "But the man who thinks about his religion will not find it always the same. Like fish in the stream it not only changes but it may come and go... It is plain that he must live a much more adventurous life of the spirit than do the devoutly unthinking"
>
> *(Wieman 1928:37-38).*

While I do not wish to paint a hard-and-fast rule here, but after 40+ years in ministry in Australia—the last 20 of those working in an overt and intentional way within 'progressive religion'—I have tried to keep Wieman's wisdom in mind and allow it to influence my liturgies and my preaching. Yes, his wisdom as well as the wisdom and courage of many 'progressive' scholars whose ideas, suggestions, and stories are reflected and propagated in these pages. My encouragement to you, my reader, is for their efforts to be explored further. Because a progressive faith is open both to expansion as well as given to definition. Both provide a sense of identity as well as room for change.

So welcome to the shards of a career, mostly 'against the stream'.

I do not see myself as an original thinker but perhaps as a reasonably good editor, able to weave thoughts, stories and ideas together in a fairly conversational, and at times, narrative way. Thus in my preaching style I try to invite others to both get curious and excited about what they hear, and to explore further. If that happens then I feel I have been faithful to my calling as a communicator, as well as being respectful of my hearer as she comes to her own conclusions.

What follows in this collection of Reflections or Sermons has been written or preached over ten years, between the years 2002 and 2012, many of them delivered in Canberra—the national capital of Australia and the centre of Federal politics—at The Church of St James, "a rainbow of Uniting, Catholic, Anglican, Lutheran, Baptist, Assembly of God, 'church alumni', Home church, Greek Orthodox; young and older, abled and differently abled, gay and straight" folk. Several of these sermons have been reworked, added to, or had bits removed, as they have been revisited in the editing process. All are invitations to my hearers and readers to explore, to go on a journey—in the spirit of progressive/post-liberal theology. Some touch on similar issues which can create areas of repetition.

Speaking process for a moment… They are reasonably short, as far as sermons go, because I reckon sermons should be short if they are going to be heard in our multimedia and digital society. To preach much longer than twelve minutes these days is bad communication no matter who you are!

They are not organised to follow an exegetical preaching pattern common with many preachers. Instead they have been shaped into several cameos—hopefully moving horizontally like a map, rather than vertically like an office building. Where what is being said strikes a chord which interests or excites, rather than trying to 'shoehorn' something—ideas, doctrine, correct belief—into people.

Originally they were all prepared in what I call 'oral writing', that is, short sentences, and by imagining an A4 page divided into three or four columns.

No long lines across the page as with printed technology. That's for silent reading. But short lines zigzagging across the page, to aid sight for an oral presentation. Such a layout assists the 'eye' to more easily travel across and down the page in a diagonal fashion, yet enabling the presenter to remain connected with the audience. And remain 'sounded'. However, in the printed format of this book the column format is not so evident.

I also invite you to remember that a sermon, as an oral form of communication, is part of a larger liturgy, a 'happening'. That is, there are many other words, images, stories, symbols, and music not published here—all of which helped shape the total event of the Sunday morning experience in which these sermons were first spoken.

All this is earthed in my vision of ministry:

• Awakening others to the best/latest contemporary religious scholarship currently available, allowing that scholarship to shape liturgies, sermons, prayers and hymns;

• Shaping services of celebration, especially the Sunday morning experience, which blend tradition with the contemporary, using inclusive language, story, conversation, Australian images and new metaphors—all from a progressive/post-liberal theological perspective;

• Inviting others to focus on a theology which advocates:
    (i) Creativity God as expressed within religious naturalism;
    (ii) the humanity of Jesus; and
    (iii) an ethical and social stance that values compassion and social justice;

• Encouraging all to push theological boundaries—to re-imagine, reconceive and reconstruct, rather than just restate.

I am grateful for the assistance given me in the preparation of this collection: to John W Smith, Dr Nigel Leaves, Dr Margaret Mayman, David Felten, and Bruce Sanguin, for reading the text, and to Hugh McGinlay of Mosaic Press with whom I worked on my first book nearly 20 years ago.

Finally, I have dedicated this book to my spouse Dylis, with much love and gratitude, and to the people of the Church of St James, in Canberra ACT, with whom I had the privilege of being their parish minister for nearly ten years.

May this book be a contribution in response to the oft heard cry:
why weren't we told!

Rex A. E. Hunt
August 2012

**Notes:**


Thompson, G. "'Well, that's just your perspective': Guarding and declaring the right understanding of the faith in a relativist culture" in *Uniting Church Studies 17*, 2, 17-32.

Wieman, H. N. *The Wrestle Of Religion With Truth*. New York: The Macmillan Company, 1928.

# Preface

## Progressive Christianity: From an Ancient Understanding of Faith into Some New Possibilities

A progressive shaping of Christianity is not new in Australia. In one form or another it has been around for 170 years or so. What is new about its current expression now directly called 'progressive', is this open and inclusive faith is 'coming out' or resurfacing in hundreds of congregations in mainline churches in Australia, and thousands around the world, as a dynamic grassroots movement.

In this article I wish to briefly introduce some of the heroes of the early and current liberal or progressive movements in Australia while outlining the characteristics and quality of the contemporary expression. This will act as the matrix for the progressive Christianity expressed in a collection of personal sermons that follow.

### Progressive Forerunners and Heroes

Two of the most celebrated liberal theological thinkers in Australia are The Revd Dr Charles Strong (1844-1942), former minister of Scots Church, Melbourne, and, later, minister of The Australian Church, Melbourne; and Revd Dr Samuel Angus (1881-1943), Professor of New Testament and Church History at St Andrew's College, Sydney, from 1915-1943.

Charles Strong described his theology as "broad or liberal" which, he claimed, was "absolutely necessary to a minister of the gospel in order to the development of a healthy Christian life" *(Badger 1971:51)*. Such a theology had several characteristics:

(i) it was fluid;
(ii) thinks of God as an indwelling, energising Spirit;
(iii) God was manifested in Humanity – Humanity was God's 'Son';
(iv) love and justice were always working together;
(v) allied itself with science; and
(vi) is based on human experience rather than an infallible book *(Badger 1971:285)*.

This stance unnerved his evangelical colleagues in the Presbyterian Church of Victoria, so attempts were taken to charge him with heresy for "promulgating and publishing heretical and unsound doctrine" *(McEachran)*.

A 'classics' scholar, Samuel Angus soon found his academic staff at St Andrew's, 'conservative'. Following the higher criticism of the European liberal thinker Harnack, he contrasted 'the religion of Jesus' with 'the religion about Jesus', believed the original message and figure of the historical Jesus could be discerned through a critical study of the New Testament, and questioned the historicity of the virgin birth, the physical resurrection and ascension, and the theory of the atonement, forming *The Heretics Club* in 1916.

He was charged with heresy—the holding of doctrine 'contrary to straight thinking'—by the Sydney Presbytery of the Presbyterian Church of New South Wales, but the 'trial' which was to last over ten years, was never concluded, provoking one commentator to say that such cases illustrate the fallacy of trying to determine theological truth by the votes of the majority.

Others who have either pre-dated or followed Strong and Angus include:

• Catherine Spence (1825-1910) came to South Australia from Scotland in 1839. A feminist Unitarian, Spence is recognised as 'the greatest Australian woman' and given the epitaph 'Grand Old Woman of Australia'. She is commemorated on the Australian five dollar note, printed in 2001 and issued for the centenary of Federation.

• Englishman George T. Walters (1853-1926) was appointed minister at the Melbourne Unitarian Christian Church at Eastern Hill in 1884. He embraced David Strauss' biblical criticism and Darwin's theory of natural selection, rejected the Trinity and the doctrine of 'eternal torment', and established a theological journal *Modern Thought* in which to publish his different views.

A gifted and eloquent preacher, his congregation became increasingly uneasy about his secular interests and his radical political and theological views. When in 1888, the church committee reinstated the Lord's Prayer in the service, Walters resigned in protest and moved to Sydney to the Hyde Park Unitarian Church.

• London born Alfred Sykes (1871-1940) arrived in Adelaide in 1904 and was appointed minister of Stow Memorial Congregational Church. Flinders University historian David Hilliard writes of Sykes:

> "In Adelaide, Sykes was the first to expound from the pulpit the ideas of R. J. Campbell's The New Theology (1907), a book that in England had triggered a storm of controversy on a scale that was not repeated until the publication of John Robinson's Honest to God in 1963" *(Hilliard 2006:5).*

His interest in developing a 'deep church' led him to emphasis liturgy, while at the same time he remodelled Stow Memorial by creating a raised sanctuary with a central Communion Table, and had the pulpit moved from its central position to the side.

Finally, a couple of second-generation progressives. A theological student at Leigh Methodist College, Sydney, in the 1930s, Dudley Hyde (1908-2004) was never far from institutional trouble. During his student days he was even suspended from studies because of his liberal or 'modernist' beliefs.

In 1974, twenty years before he retired and wrote his book *Rescuing Jesus From The Church*, Hyde wrote an article called 'Church guilty of gigantic Watergate coverup' for Ted Noffs' *Journal of Values (November 1974).* In that article Hyde said:

> "We ministers have seen through the absurdities and lies and contradictions and fallacies of Methodist theology for forty years but we have never been game to tell our congregations.We have known for forty years that half the stories in the Old Testament and the miracle stories of Jesus and the Virgin Birth and the Physical Resurrection were simply not 'true' in any sense in which the ordinary man understands the word 'true'" *(Ward 1996:47)*

That is, while academic theology may be able to provide an honest theology ***for*** the churches, Hyde claimed it was the theology of ministers in the pulpit who needed to offer an honest theology ***in*** the churches.

It is also interesting to note in his 'Suggestions for Further Reading', published in *Rescuing Jesus…*, Hyde said to his readers:

"... if you ever become completely involved and want to read the latest, most scholarly publication on the actual teachings and saying of Jesus read: Jesus Seminar. The Five Gospels..." *(Hyde 1994:138).*

While across the Tasman, Sir Lloyd Geering (1918-)—born in New Zealand but lived and taught in both Australia and New Zealand—is best remembered for his high-profile 1967 heresy trial within the Presbyterian Church of New Zealand, following a series of articles published in the church paper, *Outlook*. The article that caused a major storm was on the Resurrection, where he focused on a challenging statement by Ronald Gregor Smith in his book, *Secular Christianity*:

"...we may freely say that the bones of Jesus lie somewhere in Palestine. Christian faith is not destroyed by this admission. On the contrary, only now, when this has been said, are we in a position to ask about the meaning of the resurrection as an integral part of the message concerning Jesus" *(Quoted in Geering 2006:133).*

A former principal of the Theological Hall and now Professor Emeritus of Religious Studies at Victoria University, Wellington, Geering survived those charges to develop his thinking in ways that have made him New Zealand's premier progressive Christian religious thinker. He continues as a Fellow of the Westar Institute/Jesus Seminar.

Such is the growth of these modern 'progressive' movements, many can now name those overseas who are closely linked with them: Robert Funk, John Shelby Spong, Marcus Borg, Lloyd Geering, Gretta Vosper, Richard Holloway, John Dominic Crossan, and the 'Jesus Seminar' of the American Westar Institute. But there continues to be significant contributions by some outstanding locals: Val Webb, Charles Birch, Norman Habel, Margaret Mayman, Gregory Jenks, Michael Morwood, Nigel Leaves, Noel Preston, Keith Rowe, and Francis Macnab, as well as from the poets and hymn writers: Shirley Erena Murray, William Wallace, and Colin Gibson.

The movement itself does not have any structured leadership. However, national bodies or networks are forming and international events happening. Neither is its 'coming out' a response to:

> "an overarching collaboration among the various religious bureaucracies. Rather... [its membership comes] from an unorganized but broad-ranging kind of Christian response to felt needs for vital spirituality, intellectual integrity, new ways of expressing gender, an alternative to Christian sense of superiority, and a desire to act more justly in relationship to the marginalized" *(Taussig 2006:2-3).*

Three books from the many published in the last 20+ years, have almost become a manifesto for progressive Christianity: Marcus Borg's *The Heart of Christianity*, Jack Spong's *Why Christianity Must Change Or Die*, and Matthew Fox's *Original Blessings*. While a DVD collection of studies under the title *'Living the Questions'* launched by David Felten and Jeff Procter-Murphy, is now seen as a progressive alternative to the evangelical and fundamentalist material available. Likewise, is the even newer DVD series, *'The Challenge of Jesus'* by Dom Crossan.

Some of those who make up the movements in Australia at their grassroots are involved in mainline or old-line churches: Catholic, Anglican, Uniting, Lutheran—where they are often a minority in a local congregation. But many are not. These other people come from the growing ranks of the disillusioned, those who 'love the Christ and leave the Church' as New Zealand songwriter Shirley Erena Murray puts it. Or who hold membership in the 'church alumni' as Jack Spong describes it.

From my experience, it is by and large a grassroots 'lay' movement with a lesser number of ordained ministers or priests able or interested in joining—although over the past couple of years this is slowly changing as progressive clergy establish discussion groups and invite other clergy folk to join in, and as the Westar Institute and The Center for Progressive Christianity USA develop closer ties. The movement itself stands in sharp contrast to the Christianity that usually gets the majority of media coverage both here and overseas: those called conservative evangelicals and fundamentalists. To this end, the establishment of a recent 'lobby' group—Progressive Christian Voice (Australia), in Brisbane, Queensland—is to be welcomed. It seeks to address this issue of in-balance in a direct way, offering a 'progressive' voice on social and policy issues to politicians as well as to the media.

The main progressive religious groups which we now know of in Australia, include:

Progressive Christianity Network, South Australia
The Centre for Progressive Religious Thought, Canberra
The Centre for Progressive Religious Thought, Sydney
Progressive Spirituality Network, Brisbane
Australian Reforming Catholics
Progressive Christian Network of Victoria
Perth Progressives Network of Western Australia
Sea of Faith—both in Australia and New Zealand.

Along with a growing number of smaller informal groups, both in Australia and of late, in New Zealand *(Smith 2012).*

The Aim of one of these Australian groups is:

• to be a forum that explores progressive religion and spirituality in a way that provides a safe place for those who have found organised religion irrelevant, unresponsive, repressive or damaging.

And it tries to be that as it:

• Builds a network of support for those who seek to discover and live by a progressive faith, sharing ideas and pursuing questions and answers.

• Creates an open and welcoming community which respects the faith position of all participants, and encourages authentic interfaith engagement.

• Promotes progressive religious thought as an agent of change and renewal in faith communities and society.

• Links with other groups and Centres of progressive religious thought.

**Characteristics of the Movements**

In his book *A New Spiritual Home. Progressive Christianity At The Grassroots*, American New Testament scholar Hal Taussig lists five characteristics of progressive Christianity:

1. A spiritual vitality and expressiveness,
2. An insistence on Christianity with intellectual integrity,
3. A transgression of traditional gender boundaries,
4. The belief that Christianity can be vital without claiming to be the best or the only true religion,
5. Strong ecological and social justice commitments.

Let me briefly expand that list.

**1. A spiritual vitality and expressiveness**
The wide range of churches and groups express themselves spiritually in meditation, prayer, artistic forms, and participatory worship. They often reclaim discarded ancient Christian rituals and use a wide variety of non-Christian rituals and meditation techniques.

**2. An insistence on Christianity with intellectual integrity**
This new kind of Christian expression is nourished by a wide-ranging intellectual curiosity and critique. It interrogates Christian assumptions and traditions in order to reframe, reject, or renew them.

**3. A transgression of traditional gender boundaries**
These groups are explicitly and thoroughly committed to feminism and affirmation of gay, lesbian, bisexual, and transgender people.

**4. The belief that Christianity can be vital without claiming to be the best or the only true religion**
Progressive Christians take pains to claim simultaneously their own Christian faith and their support of the complete validity of other religions.

**5. Strong ecological and social justice commitments**
This movement is committed to social justice, peace advocacy as well as having a passion for environmentalism.

Generally speaking, progressive Christianity seeks:

• to provide local, open, inclusive and safe places where pushing theological boundaries is encouraged; and

• to encourage people to understand themselves uniquely sacred within the context of the sacredness of creation.

As such, much of the traditional doctrines, statements of faith, creeds and biblical understandings are questioned or rejected. So, with the aid of some broad brush strokes, what might a 'progressive' Christianity look like…

**1. Christianity**

From early days, there was not one unified group or vision called 'Christianity'—not its original title. There were several. Separate, often not knowing of others' existence. And when these different visions met, it was often a clash! For instance, the clashes between Paul and Peter over the very nature of what it means to be 'on the Way', continued to rage in one form or another, from group to group, for nearly three hundred years.

> "Since the fourth century, Christians, in the main, have championed Paul's view... [And] since Paul and his disciples wrote virtually half of the New Testament, it is little wonder that modern Christians regard the Jewish Christians as the 'villains' in the story" *(Hedrick 2006:5).*

'It'... did not begin as a separate organisation but came "to birth on the margins of the Jewish cumulative tradition..." *(Geering 2000: 143).*

A new era of biblical scholarship on Christian origins has recently opened up within progressive scholarship, and some propositions have already been offered and tested by the 'Jesus Seminar on Christian Origins':

> Did Christianity begin with what is called 'the resurrection'? No.
> Did Christianity begin with Pentecost? No.
> Did Christianity begin with Jesus? No.

Stephen Patterson, one of the scholars, reports:

> "The Fellows rejected the simple proposition that 'Christianity began with Jesus', but... endorsed the thesis... that Christianity began when Jesus used imaginative language to call into question his received life world in favor of the life world that emerges in his parables and aphorisms. In other words, Christianity began with the preaching of Jesus" *(Patterson 2007:19, 20).*

The cultures and communities in which the Jesus Movement arose were essentially oral. People learned mainly by hearing. Therefore, tradition was not a fixed thing as it is in cultures shaped by writing or print or even the electronic media. It is very fluid, passed on as talk and imagination, from generation to generation.

Oral storytellers do not ordinarily remember exact wording. Knowledge is shaped by memory. Not memory mindlessly regurgitated, but memory rethought *(Boomershine 1988)*. As storyteller and scholar David Rhoads says:

> "Most...did not memorize. They put their own stamp on the composition and adapted it to audience and circumstance" *(Rhoads 2010:8)*.

While Jesus Seminar scholar Brandon Scott is a bit more direct: *"in oral communities purveyors of the tradition freely omitted, invented, modified, enlarged" (Scott 1988:3)* their stories, layering and stitching them together to conserve tradition in an episodic manner.

Scott goes on to say:

> "The question for scholars [today] is how to distinguish these levels of talk, and especially, how to isolate Jesus' talk about the kingdom from other levels of talk in the written records, which is all we now have" *(Scott 1988:4)*.

Jesus/Yeshua wrote nothing. He spoke Aramaic and very possibly some Greek. But we don't know if he could speak Hebrew. His words have been preserved only in the Greek. Our biblical stories portray him as one who speaks rather than as one who writes.

In reality, the 'historical' Jesus of Nazareth contributed very little to what finally emerged as orthodox Christianity! *(Funk 2006:183)*.

**2. God**

God is not a supernatural being outside of the universe. Neither is the word G-o-d the proper name of a supernatural being. It is a metaphor used to address the sacred in life, often, but not exclusively, using anthropocentric language.

And it is the term used more often than any other to identify the sacred or "the ultimate in reality and value and meaning for humans" *(Kaufman 2004:1)*. Progressives accept that the biblical texts have been the most influential source of Christian and western thought about God. But not the exclusive source.

As a progressive I understand and experience 'G-o-d' as a universal creative process, continuously at work in the world, in the ordinary, giving rise to new forms of existence. Thus the metaphor I find helpful in speaking about the sacred is "serendipitous creativity" *(Kaufman 2004:42)* as suggested by theologian Gordon Kaufman. Kaufman says:

> "The concept of creativity... enables us to connect important theological concerns with central features of modern/post-modern thinking about the cosmos, the evolution of life, and the emergence of bio-historical development of human life and culture on planet Earth" *(Kaufman 2004:76)*.

Thus its features are expressed and experienced in three strands or trajectories:

> creativity 1—cosmic evolution
> creativity 2—biological evolution
> creativity 3—cultural/symbolic evolution.

He writes:

> "We do not know why or how creativity comes about: it is a profound mystery. The mark that identifies the occurrence of creativity is its consequences: something strikingly new, something transformative has come into being and has become a significant feature of the ongoing world" *(Kaufman 2006: xiv)*.

**3. Jesus/Yeshua**

Jesus/Yeshua was a homeland Jew not a Christian. Deeply real. Intensely human. He never rejected his Jewish roots. He made no theological statements. Neither did he set out to establish a new religion, appoint clergy or inaugurate celibacy. Although it appears he did encounter opposition to his perception of religion and reality from the authorities of the day, just how hostile this opposition was, is a matter of speculation.

As a wandering secular Galilean sage, Jesus/Yeshua belonged more to the 'wisdom' stream than the 'priestly' stream of Judaism. His language is indirect and highly metaphorical, while the primary avenues of access to him come from the synoptic gospels (Mark, Matthew, Luke) and the Gospel of Thomas. But it must also be noted: they are not neutral accesses.

Progressive thinking distinguishes between the historical Jesus (pre-Easter Jesus) who lived in a particular time and place, and the mythical Christ (post-Easter Christ). In the traditional Church the 'historical' Jesus is smothered by superimposing the heavenly figure of Christ on him *(Funk & Hoover 1993:7)*.

> "Jesus is displaced by the Christ, as the so-called Apostles' Creed makes evident... Nothing between his birth and death appears to be essential to his mission or to the faith of the church"
>
> *(Funk & Hoover 1993:7).*

Some of the best, I reckon, current progressive Christian scholarship comes from the Westar Institute and its various seminars—primarily the Jesus Seminar and its search for the 'historical Jesus'. Its founder, Robert Funk *(Funk 2000)* compiled a short list of insights about Jesus. Among them he listed:

(i) Jesus as sage, teaching orally,
(ii) trust is the horizon of the kingdom,
(iii) kinship in the kingdom,
(iv) celebration rather than apocalyptic,
(v) humour, humility and morality,
(vi) the cross as symbol of integrity.

The Seminar's work is a continuing process of reconstruction as it attempts, with imagination, to piece together the fragments of Jesus' vision among the words attributed to him. Not to try and discover the exact words or thoughts but, as Gregory Jenks says, that:

> "we may just discover what we need to do about [an] issue. And that, I suspect, is what Jesus wants most of all—not imitation, but a sustained effort to practice the kind of faith he seems to have found, and to live with the kind of wisdom that he seems to have embodied, and in the end to die with the kind of integrity that he seems to have demonstrated"
>
> *(Jenks 2012).*

As a result, its findings also challenge three traditional ways of understanding Jesus, that:

(i) Jesus claimed to be the incarnate Son of God who came to earth
to save us from sin,
(ii) Jesus claimed to be the Suffering Servant, and
(iii) Jesus claimed to be the apocalyptic Son of Man or an apocalyptic prophet.

In recent years, there has been less talk about a 'divine' Jesus/Yeshua, resulting in Jesus having been given a 'demotion'.

> "Such a demotion of Jesus in relationship to God has kept Jesus' value as a centrally exemplary human being, often compared with the Buddha, Mohammed, or Moses. In other words, Jesus has remained a central figure for the faith of [progressive] Christians, while becoming more human than divine" *(Taussig 2006:27)*

"Christian conviction eventually overwhelms Jesus", says Robert Funk, "he is made to confess what Christians had come to believe" *(Funk & Hoover 1993:24).*

**4. Bible**
In progressive Christianity, the Bible is not the literal Word of God. It is a human product made up of at least two collections: the Old Testament—the product of ancient Israel; and the New Testament—the product of several early Christian communities, all quite different from their modern counterparts. It includes many different images, concepts and ways of thinking about G-o-d or the sacred, while its stories arise out of many socio-cultural contexts.

Marcus Borg *(Borg 2000)* suggests five ways of re-visioning the Bible.
By 'seeing it again' as:

(i) a human product
- the product of two ancient communities

(ii) a combination of historical memory and metaphorical narratives
- some events really happened
- some, no particular event lies behind them

(iii) stories about the divine-human relationship
(iv) in a state of post-critical naiveté
- hear the stories once again as 'true' even though not 'factually true'

(v) and, as a lens and sacrament
- a way of seeing rather than an object of belief,
- in its function not its origin

The Bible also carries at least two different portraits of Jesus: one painted by John; the other painted by the synoptics—(Mark, Matthew, Luke).

> "In the synoptic gospels, Jesus speaks in brief, pithy one-liners and couplets, and in parables... In John, by contrast, Jesus speaks in lengthy discourses or monologues, or in elaborate dialogues prompted by some deed Jesus has performed" *(Funk & Hoover 1993:10).*

Both cannot be historically accurate.

**5. Non-canonical**

Non-canonical—those writings which did not make it into the accepted biblical Canon—or the so-called 'gnostic' gospels, has caused some excitement in recent years. To mention just two:

- The Gospel of Thomas:

  A collection of 114 sayings and aphorisms with no narrative framework, no account of Jesus' trial, death and resurrection, no birth or childhood stories, and no account of his public ministry. Of the sayings, 65 are unique to Thomas.

- The Gospel of Mary:

  Presents a radical interpretation of Jesus' teachings as a path to inner knowledge, rejects Jesus' suffering and death as the path to eternal life, and honours the legitimate and positive contribution of women's leadership.

Much of this excitement is due to the 1945 discovery at ancient Chenobaskian, now Nag Hammadi, some 370 miles south of Cairo, Egypt, called the Nag Hammadi Library—45 texts in thirteen papyrus books or codices—and the recent translation and interpretive work done on them by scholars. The stories around this find say a man named Muhammad Ali was looking for fertilizer for fuel and stumbled upon a clay jar containing several codices of manuscripts.

These 4th century Christian papyrus books, almost all of which were previously unknown, offer new perspectives on Christian beginnings. Beginnings which "were much more diverse then we had ever imagined" *(King 2003)*. Karen King explains:

> "Early Christians intensely debated such basic issues as the content and meaning of Jesus' teachings, the nature of salvation, the value of prophetic authority, the roles of women and slaves, and competing visions of ideal community. After all, these first Christians had no New Testament, no Nicene Creed or Apostles' Creed, no community established church order or chain of authority, no church buildings, and indeed no single understanding of Jesus" *(King 2003:1)*.

However, as history is usually written by the winners, the

> "viewpoints of the losers were largely lost since their ideas survived only in documents denouncing them. Until now" *(King 2003:1)*.

Progressive Christians study and use some of these writings in scholarly work as well as in worship services. They offer an alternative voice in ancient debate. A voice which the winners declared as 'heresy' as they sought to marginalise their impact. And then enacted their decisions through force—even death. But progressive Christians also study these writings because

> "much in Christian belief and practice rests upon historical claims [and] an accurate view of history is crucial" *(King 2003:3)*.

**6. Hymns and Creeds**

We believe what we sing. Hymns are religious artefacts created to allow us to speak of our experience of the sacred. They are also historical artefacts.

A hymn is not written to be sung once but rather a hundred, two hundred times. To become part of the familiar, often-used tradition of a living religion. But that is also reason why it is very important to sing new songs or hymns and appropriate ones at that, because those same hymns weren't written to be sung for a hundred years! Our perceptions and experience of the sacred, change. And so too should what we say and sing.

Likewise, Creeds are also religious and historical artefacts. They may link us to the 'great tradition' but they also mark thinking at a particular time. That is, they also draw boundaries, as was the experience that came out of Nicea in 325 CE, and then later when Emperor Theodosius imposed the Nicene Trinity on the Church in 381 CE at Constantinople.

> "What Theodosius achieved", writes historian Charles Freeman, "was the championing of one Christian faction over another and the strengthening of its position by ostracising its rivals, both Christian and pagan" *(Freeman 2008:200).*

Creeds always exclude. They bring debate to an end and denigrate curiosity. And in the wrong hands, become weapons of abuse. However, it is also worth noting that when a proposal from the steering committee of the Literacy and Liturgy Seminar of the Westar Institute suggested its initial project be the writing of a new creed, a clear difference of opinion was expressed by the membership. Sometimes this difference was expressed in terms of scholarship verses practitioners. Other times it was plain indifference: who would use such a creed!

**7. Prayer**

Prayer for progressive Christians is not talking to a supernatural being, Harry Potter style, hoping if one uses the right gestures or says the right words, he (traditional language and images of God are nearly always in masculine terms) will manipulate the situation for us. Neither is it Santa style—be good and get what you ask for.

For progressives, prayer could perhaps be described as poetry or the 'language of the heart'. Not just in some interior realm. Certainly not is some oral heavenly escape. But as an invitation to sense the connectedness of the whole of life—the "in-between-ness of God" *(Taussig 1999:131)*—the "always present God" rather than "an elsewhere God" *(Morwood 2003:8)*. Danish philosopher Soren Kierkegaard once commented 'prayer does not change God, but it changes him who prays'. Others have refined that a bit, to: 'Prayer doesn't change things. Prayer changes people and people change things'.

Inclusive language is used in reference to G-o-d and humankind in both prayer and meditation. And rather than an emphasis on prayer as petition, many progressives experience prayer as:

- listening in silence
- giving insights into ourselves and possibly others
- connecting us to each other and the world around us.

In a worship service, there is also often a free time for sharing joys and concerns.

**8. Worship/Sunday morning experience**

Towards the end of his life, Westar Institute founder Robert Funk, issued a 'call to arms' on worship or the Sunday morning experience:

> *"throw the old forms out and start over [again]... design a new Sunday Morning experience from the ground up... new music, new liturgy, new scriptures, new ceremonies, new rites of passage" (Funk 2005:2).*

And what goals might this 'experience' contain? Funk made a few suggestions:

(i) it should square with and thus confirm the modern world as the horizon of our bona fide religious experience;
(ii) the experience should include confession: confession of the church's moral failures;
(iii) it should have scriptures, selectively chosen, from the Bible and other sacred texts, ancient and modern;
(iv) the experience should grant permission to undertake journeys of faith into unchartered territories;
(v) be radically inclusive;
(vi) should praise new icons who have pioneered the way in new paths of trust and openness;
(vii) it should be a celebration of life; and
(viii) support the creation or identification of new music and symbols.

After more than forty years as a progressive, shaping and reshaping liturgies, I agree. I also have come to the conclusion that worship is not about the praise of G-o-d. It is about the celebration of life, the whole of life.

So my understanding of progressive worship is:

- A human activity, celebrated in the presentness of G-o-d or the Sacred. Rather than praise required of us by G-o-d or the Sacred.
- Must be broad enough to create a co-operative experience (rather than collective)—cognitively and emotionally.
- Be a celebration of whole of life (in ordinary times).
- Have form or shape.
- Use of artistic media and symbols highlights the 'art' of worship.
- Be 'landscape' and 'intellectually' honest.

And the goal of this worship or celebration? To help us know and feel how we relate as individuals to ourselves, others, the world, the universe. To celebrate that relationship. To touch sources of creative transformation. To reinterpret our experiences. To reaffirm living in this world.

The form or shape of my liturgies usually offer six encounter points: Gathering, Centering, Exploring, Affirming, Celebrating, Scattering.

But above all one's shaping of liturgy should always be WWKAWWB honest. We must go beyond the "intellectual two-step" called "latitudinarianism"—that is, preserving one's intellectual integrity by proclaiming belief beyond literalism, but continuing to use the anthropomorphic language or images of the traditional hymns, liturgy and creeds "in order to remain within the tradition" *(Loehr 2000:8).*

> "...playing this game compromises our integrity and our religion... [because] it is another example of keeping what we know and what we believe separated" *(Loehr 2000:9).*

**Continuing the Conversation**

Returning to Hal Taussig's research in the USA, he has flagged some interesting observations. Some of them are yet to be tested in Australia and New Zealand, but as I feel the pulse of those around me I am not surprised to hear similar comments here.

His observations centre on:

(i) the growth of progressive Christianity has come from the non-churched or those alienated from the church;
(ii) progressive Christianity will continue to be a small minority;
(iii) mainline Protestant denominations will almost certainly continue to decline... Indeed another is bold to add: *"they are largely too anxious about their falling numbers and dwindling cultural influence to risk additional losses at the hands of theological reform" (Bessler-Northcutt 2004:63);*
(iv) Roman Catholicism *"will continue to hollow itself" (Taussig 2006:124)*, and
(v) evangelicalism will continue to appeal, but *"its inability to relate to the life-giving character of women's rights and scientific discovery in any way but oppositional, will continue to limit [its] scope" (Taussig 2006:124).*

Progressive Christianity is not intimidated by the fact there are more numerous other kinds of Christianity around. Nor do we feel the need to enforce the truth claims of the past, often based on victories of politics and power rather than any search for truth, or to dismiss the claims of other religions simply as mistakes made by "anonymous Christians" *(Karl Rahner, quoted in Taussig 2006:171)*. But we are committed activists and advocates—often passionate ones at that.

The future of progressive Christianity in Australia and New Zealand, five, ten years from now will depend on a few more things happening:

(i) establishing intentional **biblical literacy** programs in congregations, which discern and advocate the distinctive voice of the 'historical Jesus' as a corrective or counter voice to the competitive and debilitating spirit of our times;
(ii) supporting the few **progressive scholars** in our Theological Colleges as they strive to get current biblical literacy scholarship onto the curriculum; and where necessary, establishing **parallel streams of learning** where Theological Colleges refuse to support progressive biblical literacy;
(iii) continuing the development and publication of more progressive **educational material** suitable for children, as pioneered by The Center for Progressive Christianity USA;

(iv) sharing of progressive and creative **liturgical** efforts as the 'Sunday Morning experience' is reshaped;
(v) growing a powerful 'progressive' **grassroots movement**, begun over the past 20 plus years, and
(vi) developing of a clear and sustained **national** progressive voice and profile, especially through the Common Dreams Conferences.

May it be so with us.

**Notes**:

C. R. Badger. 1971. *The Reverend Charles Strong And The Australian Church*. Melbourne: Abacada Press 1883.

Bessler-Northcutt, J. "Learning to see God. Prayer and practice in the wake of the Jesus Seminar" in R. W. Hoover (ed) *The Historical Jesus Goes To Church*. Santa Rosa: Polebridge Press, 2004.

Boomershine, T. E. *Story Journey. An Invitation To The Gospel As Storytelling*. Nashville: Abingdon Press, 1988.

Borg, M. *The Heart Of Christianity. Rediscovering A Life Of Faith*. New York. HarperCollins, 2003.

————,"Re-visioning Christianity" in R. W. Funk. (ed) *The Once And Future Jesus*. Santa Rosa: Polebridge Press, 2000.

Fox, M. *Original Blessings. A Primer In Creation Spirituality*. Santa Fe: Bear Co., 1983.

Freeman, C. *AD 381. Heretics, Pagans, and the Dawn of the Monotheistic State*. Woodstock: The Overlook Press, 2008.

Funk, R. W. & R. Hoover (ed) *The Five Gospels. The Search for the Authentic Words of Jesus*. New York: McMillan, 1993.

Funk, R. W. "Editorial" in *The Fourth R 18*, 1, 2, 20. 2005.

———— "The once and future Jesus" in R. W. Funk. (ed) *The Once And Future Jesus*. Santa Rosa: Polebridge Press, 2000.

Geering, L. *Wrestling With God. The Story Of My Life*. Exeter: Imprint Academic, 2006

————, "The legacy of Christianity" in R. W. Funk. (ed) *The Once And Future Jesus*. Santa Rosa: Polebridge Press, 2000.

Hedrick, C. W. "What is Christian? Competing visions in the first century" in *The Fourth R 19*, 4, 3-8, 22. 2006.

Hilliard, D. "Strong's liberal contemporaries: Adelaide, 1870-1914". Part of the Strong Symposium, University of South Australia. The Charles Strong Memorial Trust, 2006.

Hyde, D. *Rescuing Jesus From The Church.*Bayview: Minkara Press, 1994.
Jenks, G. C. "Imagine this: Jesus and the kingdom of God" in J. H. Ellens. (ed) *Winning Revolutions: The Psychology Of Successful Revolts For Freedom, Fairness, and Rights.* 3 Vols. Westport: Praeger, 2012.
Kaufman, G. *Jesus and Creativity.* Minneapolis: Fortress Press, 2006.
————, *In The Beginning... Creativity.* Minneapolis: Fortress Press, 2004.
King, K. "Letting Mary Magdalene speak". Web site: Beliefnet. 2003. Accessed June 2006.
Loehr, D. "Salvation by character: How UU's can find the religious center" in *Journal of Liberal Religion 1*, 2, 1-14. 2000.
McEachran, D. S. "A letter to Dr Charles Strong" in C. R. Badger. 1971. *The Reverend Charles Strong And The Australian Church.* Melbourne: Abacada Press 1883.
Morwood, M. *Praying A New Story.* Melbourne: Spectrum Publications, 2003.
Patterson, S. J. "Report from the Jesus Seminar on Christian origins" in *The Fourth R 20*, 1, 16-20. 2007.
Rhoads, D. "Scholarly Reflection: A discussion about the importance of Biblical Performance Criticism—with David Rhoads" in *The Biblical Storyteller*, Summer, 2010.
Scott, B. B. "Introduction: What did Jesus really say?" in Funk, R. W. et. al. *The Parables Of Jesus.* Red Letter Edition. The Jesus Seminar.
Santa Rosa: Polebridge Press, 1988.
Smith, J. W. H. "Progressive Christianity: A grassroots response" in Hunt,
R. A. E. & J. W. H. Smith. (ed) *We Weren't Told! A Handbook On Progressive Christianity.* Salem: Polebridge Press, 2012.
Spong, J. S. *Why Christianity Must Change Or Die. A Bishop Speaks To Believers In Exile.* NY: New York. HarperCollins, 1998.
Taussig, H. *A New Spiritual Home. Progressive Christianity At The Grassroots.* Santa Rosa: Polebridge Press, 2006.
————, *Jesus Before God. The Prayer Life Of The Historical Jesus.* Santa Rosa: Polebridge Press, 1999.
Ward, W. *Men Ahead Of Their Time.* Melbourne: The Joint Board of Christian Education, 1996.

# Stay Alert! Advent 'Incarnation' from the Landscape

Advent 1, 2008
Mark 13:33-37

"Christmas break-up parties, cash registers and last minute rush of buying presents, department store window displays, Xmas cards, glitter, tinsel, fake snow and days gearing up for summer, test cricket, holiday plans, end of a weary year.
It is all too familiar and it happens every year.
And yet amid all this excitement, anticipation and frenetic activity 'drummed up' by the commercial world there is...
'the muffled drumbeat of Advent'"
*(Smith 1986:1).*

The Church has its own calendar of seasons.
And in that calendar a new liturgical year begins today,
the first Sunday in Advent.

So the biblical readings have changed, especially the gospel readings.
From today we begin to hear an emphasis on Mark's stories.
And a new contemporary symbolic colour is in evidence—blue,
rather than the traditional Advent colour—purple.

All of this is picked up in a resource collection we call the Lectionary.
The Revised Common Lectionary to be exact.
About that Lectionary I want to make some observations.

oo0oo

For those of us who live in the southern hemisphere
the Lectionary is primarily a foreign document.
A northern hemisphere document to be exact.
And that's our liturgical problem.

In the Lectionary each of the Church seasons were originally aligned
to the seasonal changes of the northern hemisphere natural year.

For instance, Easter is a northern spring festival of new life.
But in the southern hemisphere Easter occurs in autumn,

a season of change, of 'little deaths',
as leaves—millions of them—fall from 'northern' trees.

While Christmas, as many cards show, is a northern,
primarily indoors, midwinter festival,
urging the return of the sun.

But in Australia Christmas is a midsummer outdoors festival
in the midst of the heat and glare of the sun,
often bush fires, and usually blow flies.

I have tried for many years to do a reshape and a rethink
on the traditional Church seasons.
But powerful controlling conservative ecumenical forces
have prevented any serious rethinking or reshaping
of the Lectionary, from a southern hemisphere perspective.

The only small dent that has been put in this fortress mentality
has been the new Season of Creation, a southern hemisphere initiative,
but it comes within the Season After Pentecost.

So we seem stuck with the overall Lectionary ancient cosmology
and seasonal irrelevance!

Australian poet Les Murray has said that
the four traditional seasons of the northern world
are the greatest and most significant cultural import
Australians have seen.

I agree.

Similarly, Sydney priest David Ranson has suggested that by limiting
ourselves to a cultural colonialism with northern or European origins,
we risk missing or not seeing what actually 'is'.

As in the Central Highlands (Victoria) from early-August:
local wattles—bright yellow and rich gold—start to bloom
heralding a new dawn after winter's inactivity.

As in the Central West (NSW) from mid-November:
the smell of drying earth and blossom
fills our nostrils with bursts of Jacaranda royal purple.

Perhaps Australian poet Judith Wright has the clue
to our institutional reluctance.

In the 'Introduction' to *A Book of Australian Verse* she writes:

> "For many years, a conception of Australia as a country to be loved and valued for its own sake was rare and difficult to uphold... What did arise... was, not a love of the country as such, but rather of the freedom its great distances provided" *(Wright 1968:2).*

So in all seriousness, I reckon we should take the brave step of moving
away from the traditional 'northern' four seasons mode
and seek to replace them with celebrations
which are aligned to what happens where we are.
To what 'is'.

oo0oo

In the early 1980s we moved from Creswick,
in the Central Highlands of Victoria, to the Western District, to Colac, Victoria.
And very quickly I discovered that one of our near neighbours
was John Wheeler of *Five Australian Christmas Carols* fame.

I remember the first time I sung *'Carol of the Birds'* in St Andrew's.
It was magnificent!

"Out on the plains the Brolgas are dancing
Lifting their feet like war-horses prancing:
Up to the sun the wood-larks go winging
Faint in the dawn light echoes their singing -
Orana! Orana! Orana! to Christmas Day" *(Wheeler 1948).*

Our UCA hymnbook, *Together in Song*, also has the James/Wheeler classic,
*'The North Wind...'.*

A couple of years after I was discovering my near neighbour,
Professor James Tulip proposed to the then Australian Council of Churches
that it conduct a national competition for an
Australian Christmas carol. He wrote:

"The failure of imagination to see what is there close at hand
as spiritual resources in Australia is particularly obvious at Advent."

He then went on to suggest:

"Advent in Australia is the time when… the angophoras or red gums around Sydney… are a revelation of subtle colouring as their old bark peels off. It is as if a great silent ritual is taking place—like the Three Kings bringing their gold, frankinsense and myrrh—as a tribute for the divine at-oneness with the world, which is the meaning of Christmas" *(Tulip 1985:4).*

The winning entry was submitted by Jeff Guess
who offered these new images:

"Come, see the light break, come watch the sun
Here on this new day, Christmas begun,
Start from the dark branch, crown of a King,
Flowers of purple blossom and cling.
*Melaleuca morning mantle*
*Cascades from heat and from night*
*Bears upon its royal holly*
*Birth of peace and love and light*" *(Guess 1986).*

Since those days others have also composed new,
more radical southern hemisphere hymns.
And they are beginning to be sung in many congregations
in Australia and New Zealand.

One which is most appropriate, I reckon,
is written by Shirley Erena Murray:

"Carol our Christmas,
an upside down Christmas;
snow is not falling and
trees are not bare.
Carol the summer, and
welcome the Christ Child,
warm in our sunshine and

sweetness of air" *(Murray 1993).*
By limiting ourselves to a cultural colonialism with northern origins,
we risk missing or not seeing what actually 'is'.

oo0oo

Advent is the beginning of a new year. A new Church year.
But with a beginning there is also an ending.
An ending of a year.

And for some, if not for many, the past year has been a difficult year:

- wars have continued,
- bank closures on family homes have left people with shattered dreams,
- the gap between rich and poor continues to grow.

Closer to home in our own suburb:

- Loved ones got ill.
- Some moved away, or died.
- Others become unemployed.

And all of us continued to struggle with 'the vicissitudes of time'.

So, as an overseas colleague asks: where's the 'good news'?
The answer to that question is exactly where it has always been.
In and among us.

For me part of that 'good news' this Advent
is to become more aware of, more sensitive to,
the God-given moments in our ordinary daily events,
despite all the seasonal advertising over-load.
Especially as these moments sneak up on us, almost incognito,
in the landscape of this southern hemisphere land—in all its diversity.

Our anonymous gospel storyteller of mysteries and warnings
whom we call Mark, has set one scene for this new year: 'Stay awake!'
Ears tuned.
Eyes open.
Aware of.
Sensitive to.

Not to some supposed terrorist threat or 'heavenly' future event or time.
But to now, the present moment, in this place, among this people.
Engaging meaningfully in life.
Your life.

Buddhist monk, Thich Nhat Hanh, says:
"Waking up this morning, I smile. Twenty four brand new hours are before me. I vow to live fully in each moment and to look at all beings with eyes of compassion" *(Quoted in Earth Prayers).*

oo0oo

Advent in the southern hemisphere
is a time to be surprised by the ordinary
and empowered by the symbolic
as we re-imagine the world.

For Advent is a time to discover the God-given moments
in our ordinary daily events:
• in the click-clack of two branches knocking together in the wind...
• in the realisation that rain is not a singular thing
but made up of billions of individual drops of water,
each with its own destination and timing...
• in the flares of a friend's passion to shape justice
with a new vision of 'commonwealth'...
• in the love-making songs of the Green Grocer cicadas…

These are Advent moments. These are sacred moments.
Sensing the presentness of Creativity God
in the ordinary and the symbolic.
May we have the wisdom to see and honour,
understand and celebrate, this Advent!

**Notes:**

*Carol Our Christmas. A Book Of New Zealand Carols*. Raumati: New Zealand Hymnbook Trust, 1996.

Guess, J. "Melaleuca Morning" in *In Unity*. The Australian Council of Churches newsletter, November 1986.

Roberts, E. & E. Amidon. *Earth Prayers From Around The World. 365 Prayers, Poems, And Invocations For Honoring The Earth*. New York: HarperCollins, 1991.

Smith, M. "A plea for Christmas, a plea for Advent" in *The Summit 13*, 4, 1-4. 1986.

Tulip, J. "An Australian Advent" in *In Unity*. The Australian Council of Churches newsletter, November, 1985.

Wheeler, J. *Five Australian Christmas Carols*. London: Chappell & Co, 1948.

Wright, J. (ed). *A Book Of Australian Verse*. Melbourne: Oxford University Press, 1968.

# A Defiant Christmas as A Sign of Hope

Christmas Eve, 2007
Luke 2:1-14

This Christmas, as with every Christmas,
we are invited to hear again an age-old story
in new and creative ways.

That's what makes preaching on Christmas Eve
and Christmas Day so challenging for ministers.
Because most of us have heard the story so often
it is almost impossible to experience any surprising novelty.

So it was with an amount of delight when I discovered
a few years back, William (Bill) Loader's reflection:
"Christmas in a time of fiscal restraint".

It has a somewhat 'bureaucratic' ring to it!
But as we are in Canberra—the National Capital—perhaps you too
will be able to resonate with both its
humour and its indirect suggestiveness.

'When Quirinius was governor of Syria,
the administration of the empire was facing fiscal restraint
and urgent need for a strategic review of resources.

'However the planned census
failed to pass the committee stages of the senate
with the result that the census was confined
to Judea in Palestine.

'This would benefit the government
by leading to the laying off of 85,000 staff,
many of whom would starve to death,
leading, in turn,
to significant savings in welfare payments.

'The federal bureau of resource economics
had proved beyond doubt that
people who were either dead
or too infirm to make the trip to the sources of relief
produced a negative impact on demand
resulting in the likelihood of an improved surplus...'
*(Loader 2002).*

Any resemblance to well known government agencies is only accidental!

In similar creative vein is the imaginative suggestion by Jack Shea,
an American, priest, theologian and excellent storyteller.

Seven years ago in a radio talk, he said that if he was really game
he would like to send out Christmas cards
which had, on the cover, three images.

A star, brightly shining but surrounded by darkness.
An evergreen tree, but surrounded by trees without leaves.
A child wrapped in swaddling clothes and laid in a manger,
but surrounded by a ramshackle stable.
"[And] when you open the card, inside there will be in very bold print,
'Have a defiant Christmas!'" *(Shea. 2000).*

So let me stay with Jack's Christmas card for a few minutes
and briefly explore his suggested images.

1. A light shining, but shining in the darkness.
"Christmas isn't about light," Jack reflected, "[i]t's about light in the darkness... There is a defiance to the light. It lives in the darkness but the darkness cannot overcome it" *(Shea 2000).*

2. An evergreen tree surrounded by trees without leaves.

Remembering Jack lives in the northern hemisphere, he says:

"In the seeming dead of winter when all the other trees lose their leaves, the evergreens stay green and stay awake. The evergreens are defiant. They defy the defoliage of winter. They live and they give us a sense of life" *(Shea 2000).*

3. A child wrapped in swaddling clothes and laid in a manger.
Being wrapped in swaddling clothes means the child is loved.
The child is not abandoned, but taken care of.

But it happens in a place where there is no room for them at the inn.
Where there is no hospitality.
In the midst of a sense of belovedness,
there is also a sense of defiance.

Three images.
The light shines but it defies the darkness as it shines.
The bush is green, but it defies the loss of leaves in winters.
The child is beloved but it defies a sense of rejection and inhospitality.

Jack concluded his radio talk:

"But I suppose we really don't want a card like that. We want a card that is all light or all greenness or all love, but I do not think it is always the condition we are in when we celebrate Christmas" *(Shea 2000).*

Following the program the producer spoke with Jack and asked him a series of questions based on his presentation.

He went on to explain:

"People would often [say]... Christmas is about hope. But then as soon as you say [that], and you look at your own life or the larger world and all the things that beset us, you wonder. Do you just look and do an estimate of situations and say, 'Well, I can have a little hope but not a lot of hope?' Or does hope come from a different dimension of us? So I began to ponder the Christmas story as a story of hope because it could defy the negative circumstances that afflict us individually and socially, too, and it proclaimed hope that way. So I took the path of hope to be a path of defiance of negative circumstances" *(Shea 2000).*

Gee, I resonate with that!

oo0oo

Tonight, you are I gather here, aware of our own lives
and aware of events in the larger world,
as much as we can experience it.

We don't forget all we've seen on TV, or heard on radio,
or read in the newspapers, or personally experienced
over the past 12 months or so.

So how can we celebrate?
It seems to me Christmas Eve is a challenge to celebrate the birth
of healing and new possibilities, defiantly!

"The season asks us to get inside of our experience," suggests Tari Lennon, "not just talk about it or interpret it—which alters it, but simply be inside our experience. To be inside our experience is to understand that merely repeating the stories of our spiritual ancestors, or rehearsing rituals in their honor, or clinging to our own traditions, how ever precious they might be, is not the same as living our experience. For me, this year, my living experience will be enlarged by two friends who are pressing through the bleak mid-winter of dire news [about cancer] to light advent candles trusting that their vulnerabilities and God's meet in the birth of the infant Jesus" *(Lennon 2007).*

Merry Christmas.
Be blessed.
Be courageous.
Be defiant!

**Notes:**

Loader, W. "Reflections". Personal website. http://wwwstaff.murdoch.edu.au/~loader/xmas.html Accessed 2002. Used with permission of the author.

Shea, J. Presentation. 30 Good Minutes Web site, 2000. Accessed via *The Text This Week*, http://www.textweek.com/ Accessed 2007).

Lennon, T. "Lectionary Resources" Process & Faith web site. http://processandfaith.org/resources/lectionary-commentary, Accessed December 2007

# Have Yourself a Very, Merry, 'Political' Christmas

Christmas Day, 2010
Luke 2:8-20

This year has certainly been the Year of Politics in Australia!
(My list...)

• Around the time of the federal election the eZine magazine *Matilda.com* wrote: "...a leadership spill that toppled a sitting prime minister, installed Australia's first female PM and saw a Labor Left candidate—endorsed and installed by the Right—signal a major policy shift to appease big business" *(MCordell, 25/6/2010).*

• Cardinal George Pell and the *Australian Christian Lobby* led by Jim Wallace once again joined forces in the public square—this time to advocate Christians not vote for the so-called 'anti-Christian' Greens, who the Cardinal described as 'sweet camouflaged poison'...

• The lobby group *GetUp* successfully challenged, on Constitutional grounds, the former Howard Government's changes to the Electoral Act, which limited the time people had to enroll to vote after an election was called. As a result a further 98,100 names were added to the roll of voters...

• Reflecting on the lead-up to the election, Andrew Hamilton consulting editor of another eZine magazine, *Eureka Street,* wrote: "In the Federal election asylum seekers and wives or children of refugees have been made fair game. So have the young unemployed. And although Indigenous Australians have not been directly targeted, they have seen guns occasionally turned in their direction... The targeting of the deprived is not new in Australian politics. Unpopular minority groups like communists and foreigners have often been the focus of political campaigns" *(Hamilton, 19/8/2010).*

• Overall, the five-week campaign was dominated by the calculations of political professionals and by attention to the whims and prejudices of small groups of Australians in marginal electorates...

• And since the election the Federal Opposition has resolved to say 'No' to every piece of legislation tabled by the Government,
inviting some to suggest its leader, Tony Abbott,
should change his name to T**no**y Abbott!

Mmm.

I mention all this not to demonise one side of politics and sanctify the other.
But to suggest that it is within a political context
we should hear the Christmas stories.
A context not often mentioned in church, it seems.

Or put another way… the infancy narratives of old
need to be set within the modern framework of
drugs in sport,
global climate change, and
aerial 'drone' bombing raids.
They all grow from the same root: the will to control.

oo0oo

So what of Christmas? Let me share an observation or two.
Today's Christmas celebration is a date on a calendar.
A public holiday.
A 'red letter' day.
A start to holidays—sun, sand and surf!

In the biblical scheme of things, these stories are late in the tradition.
Eighty to hundred years later.

It then took nearly 400 years before the early churches decided,
mainly for reasons of control and political expediency,
to celebrate the birth of the sage Jesus/Yeshua of Nazareth
as one of its festivals.

Then another 250 years or so, again
amid great debate and various other religious practices,

for about half the churches to celebrate it on 25 December.
Which is still the case today.

And even then for the next 1200 years or so, it remained a bit of a mixed bag of both celebration and being banned, until the mid 1800s.

When its celebration became popularised and sentimentalised,
- especially through the writings of Charles Dickens,
- a poem, and then later, through
- a 30-year long advertising campaign.

These days, if you believe noisy evangelical preachers,
the really big controversy over Christmas is whether or not
commerce and extravagant spending has overturned and destroyed
the so-called 'spirit' of a Dickens-type Christmas.

Hence the pious but often equally commercial protest:
'put Christ back into Christmas'.

But are these and other claims 'fair dinkum'?
And is this what the religious infancy or nativity stories are all about?

Doug Adams was the former professor of Christianity and the Arts
at the Pacific School of Religion in California.

A great advocate of joining the arts and theology,
Adams often pointed out that in nativity scenes, many great artists
portray the child Jesus as drawing together
the full diversity of humanity.

Shepherds appear ragged and poor.
Magi or astrologers appear elegant and wealthy.
One of the Magi men is old.
Another middle aged.
And another young.
All are foreigners. And one may be black.
Closest to the child Jesus is a woman,
Mary his mother, who is visible to all.

Adams would also conclude that the so-called unrighteous
as well as the so-called righteous,
are in Jesus' company.

Now I don't have a colourful painting of a nativity scene to show you.
Least of all one done by one of the world's great artists.
But I do have some art to show you,
courtesy of an overseas colleague, John Shuck *(Shuck & Jive blog)*.

Let me paint some descriptive words to go with it.

It's a nativity scene.
It's a nativity scene in Bethlehem.
It's a gated or walled nativity scene in Bethlehem.
It's a political gated or walled nativity scene in Bethlehem.

I offer this scene for a couple of reasons.
It reminds me when my colleague Revd Gregor Henderson,
as National President of the Uniting Church,
said in his 2007 Christmas message:

> "For Israelis, the suffering comes from suicide bombers and other acts of terror... For Palestinians, the suffering from 40 years of occupation is immense. Life in the West Bank is very difficult. Unemployment is rife. Some 50% of the population is in poverty. Food parcels still have to be distributed in refugee camps, where thousands of families have lived for 60 years. The heavy restrictions placed on Palestinians by the occupation seem to be counter-productive. They may be a justified response to terrorist attacks, but the daily harassments and difficulties deepen the enmity; they do not make for peace".

He then went on to say:

> "For instance, did you know that 15 year-olds are locked up in prison for six months for throwing stones at military watch-towers? Did you know that Israel is building a segregated road system in the West Bank, so that Israelis and Palestinians won't have to travel on the same roads? Did you know there are 90 military checkpoints and 562 other obstacles (trenches, roadblocks, etc.) placed on the roads in the West Bank? It's hard to see how Palestine can develop a sustainable economy, let alone form a viable state"
> *(Henderson 2007).*

Little to nothing has changed much since then.
This year we had the Israelis attack the relief vessels trying to get into Gaza with much needed supplies, and the death of seven Turkish citizens.

Then just a couple of months later my American Rabbi friend, Arthur Waskow, wrote:

> "On 27 July this year (2010), bulldozers from the Israel Lands Administration (ILA) destroyed the Bedouin village of Al-Arakib in the Negev and began the forcible removal by some 1,500 Israeli police of over 300 Bedouin Israeli citizens, mostly children, leaving them homeless, expelled from their land, and bereft of their possessions..."

He goes on:

> "The ILA demolished their homes, sheep pens, fruit orchards and olive tree groves, so that the Jewish National Fund, which is leasing the land from the ILA, can plant a forest on their land near Beersheva" *(Waskow 2010).*

The Bedouin are not Palestinians. They are Israeli citizens!

All of these, I claim, are important clues to 'hearing' the nativity or infancy stories which the church and some religious folk hear at Christmas time.
To really hear the infancy stories of the gospels, again,
we need to hear them as political, subversive stories or parables,
with a sting in the tail.

These stories, like the gospels they overview, are fictions
rather than so-called historical fact.
They draw from a collection of legends, in the
Hebrew scriptures, and from pagan mythology, to tell their story.

They paint a word picture of the kin-dom or 'empire of God'
as opposed to the kingdom or 'empire of Rome',
and their paranoid rulers often called
'Son of God', 'Saviour of the world'...

Caesar Augustus, in the midst of storyteller Luke's palette
of bright primary colours and rejoicing.
Herod, in the midst of storyteller Matthew's palette
of somber, darker hues and political intrigue.

As colleague John Shuck suggested on his blog site:

> "According to the gospels, Jesus did not come to preach some metaphysical nonsense about life after death and secret spiritual kingdoms. He preached politics, down and dirty. 'Whose side are you on?' is the message of the Gospels. Are you on the side of the powerful and the paranoid, (in our day corporations and militaristic madness) or are you on the side of those who are adversely affected by the politics of empire?" *(Shuck 2007).*

And then:

> "Read 'em and weep, you who think Christmas is not about politics" *(Shuck 2007).*

ooOoo

Let me share with you another observation.
More than 600 years ago, a male Catholic Christian mystic
and theologian asked:

> 'What good is it to me if Mary gave birth to the son of God
> 1400 years ago and I do not also give birth to the son of God
> in my time and in my culture?'

The mystic was Meister Eckhart.
His question is still valid these long centuries later.
Because I reckon Eckhart's query is about
birthing new qualities into a waiting world that needs them.

This is both the promise and the provocative challenge
of a political (and personal) Christmas.

So this year, I join several others from the progressive religion world
in wishing you and yours a 'political' Christmas.
And I also wish you courage and understanding
as you make your political—and hopefully—imaginative decisions,
to bring about a different kind of world for everyone.

For this different kind of world is
not only about personal peace of mind, tinsel and Christmas 'pud',
it is also about political peace on earth! *(Borg & Crossan 2007:x).*

**Notes:**

Borg M. & J. D. Crossan. *The First Christmas: What The Gospels Really Teach About Jesus' Birth*. New York: HarperOne, 2007.

Roll, S. K. *Towards The Origins Of Christmas*. Kampen: Kok Pharos Publishing, 1995.

Shuck, J. "A political Christmas". Shuck&Jive blog site. http://www.shuckandjive.org/ Accessed December 2007. (This site has now been removed due to a 'hacker')

Henderson, G. "Presidents Christmas Message to the Uniting Church in Australia". 2007.

Waskow, A. The Shalom Centre web site, http://theshalomcenter.org Accessed July 2010

# Some Bells Jingle and Some Bells Toll!

Christmas 1, 2004
Matthew 2:13-23

In August 2004, US Border Patrol agents in Texas,
found a life-sized crucifix, minus the cross,
on a sandbar in the middle of the river Rio Grande.
When no-one claimed it, they donated it
to the local Catholic Church.

Since its discovery, this particular image of Jesus/Yeshua
has attracted the curious and the faithful from the local area
and from across the two countries of USA and Mexico.

Likewise, the name now given it, is also significant.
Many are calling it the 'Jesus Christ of the Undocumented'.
Because it has become a symbol of the struggles
that undocumented immigrants face when trying the reach
the so-called 'promised land of the USA'.

The statue's initial appearance in a sandbar in the middle of the Rio Grande,
is reminiscent of many Mexican immigrants' path to the US.

Some drown in the occasional torrents of the Rio Grande, trying to get to Texas.
Others die of thirst in the deserts of Arizona and New Mexico.
Some make it safely into the US
only to find themselves slaves in garment factories
or other sweatshops or, even worse,
forced into lives of prostitution.
Others are packed into container trucks and abandoned,
to suffocate in heat greater than 50 degrees celsius.
Still others are turned back at the border
and never make it very far into the US.

A few, very few, do make it, but tend to live very frugally *(TMundo)*

Tod Mundo, from whom I received this actual account,
offers these comments:

> "Jesus Christ of the Undocumented reminds Christians that Jesus suffers the indignities of the undocumented as they struggle, suffer, and sometimes die in their attempts.. (But) how do we Christians... treat the undocumented?... Do we call them by the derisive term 'wetbacks? Do we take advantage of their willingness to work cheaply and pay them substandard wages for work around our houses? Do we support politicians and policies that make their lives more difficult than they already are... by prohibiting them from getting driver's licenses or preventing their children from attending public schools? When we persecute the 'undocumented' in these and other ways, we are driving nails into the hands of Jesus himself, as the bleeding hands and brow of Jesus Christ of the Undocumented reminds us" *(Mundo 2004).*

oo0oo

Much of the story we hear during Christmas
comes from the anonymous biblical storyteller
we have given the anglo-celtic name, Luke.

In artistic terms, this is a picture full of bright primary colours.

- A cheerful story.
- A buoyant, hopeful, joyous story.

But every couple of years or so we hear a different story.
One told by the anonymous Jewish storyteller we call Matthew.

Again in artistic terms, Matthew's picture uses a darker palette.
The colours are more sombre, darker hues.

- A gothic story—disturbing, disquieting.

We also hear this 'darker palette' in Norman Habel's poem "The flight",
published in the book *Outback Christmas*,
an edited collection of poems and paintings by Habel and Pro Hart:

> "We fled into the wilderness
> like plunging through the eye
> of life's cast unseen enemy
> inviting us to die....

"Cross endless plains of burning earth
where only fierce ants fly,
sharp tongues of grass like barbed wire
invited us to die..." *(Hart & Habel 1990:44).*

We hear it in Tod Mundo's story of 'Jesus Christ of the Undocumented'.

We hear it in the Iraq tribunal hearings opened 16 days ago
(December 11, 2004) in Tokyo—a form of war crimes trials.
They speak of the deaths of an estimated 48,000 to 260,000 Iraqi citizens,
and post-war effects that could take the lives
of an additional 200,000 Iraqis.
Surely this must qualify as a genuine slaughter of the innocents!

And we hear it in the media accounts
of long term detainees at the Baxter Detention Centre in South Australia,
participating in hunger strikes in protest against their detention
and possible deportation to Iran.

Luke's story and Matthew's story are very different.
And despite attempts to the contrary
by both the church and the many 'Carols by Candlelight' events,
they can't be harmonised into one grand, neat, pious story.

Don't get me wrong. I am not against Christmas.
Indeed I am an enthusiastic supporter of the festival.
And I agree with historian Clement Miles when he says:

> "The God of Christmas is no ethereal form, no mere spiritual essence, but a very human child, feeling the cold and the roughness of the straw, needing to be warmed and fed and cherished.
>
> "Christmas is the festival of the natural body, of this world; it means the consecration of the ordinary things of life, affection and comradeship, eating and drinking and merry-making..." *(Miles 1912/76).*

But I also want to claim that the story (rather than the history) of infanticide

which is the context for the biblical story we heard this morning,
is as much a part of the Christmas story
as is the story of the baby
haloed in love and holiness,
lighting the manger with peace.

In so doing, I am seeking to acknowledge the tension many of us feel
as we try to hold on to the wonder and the magic of the Christmas season,
amid all the challenges of the ordinary, everyday.

An acknowledgement I admit,
that calls for our patience as well as active discernment!
For not all bells jingle at Christmas time. Some toll.

And if John Donne's solemn advice be right
we do not need to go too far to find out 'for whom the bell tolls!'

oo0oo

Life is never lived on a high all the time.
Christmas is not found in some rarefied sacredness.
Jesus/Yeshua might have escaped the sword of Herod,
but he died under the orders of Pilate.

I wish I had more... indeed, some, words of comfort
for the many innocent sufferers in this country and our world,
at this time.
If I knew them I would speak them.

But I do call out in solidarity, as a friend, and with hope...
Hope which was gathered up and presented to us
in the gift of a child, at Christmas.

Hope made know in the goodness born into the world
in spite of the demons that strike madly at all innocents,
past and present.

So if Christmas is not your celebration
I continue to hope rather than despair,
that Easter and its promise of new possibilities against all odds, shall be.

**Notes:**

Hart, P. & N. Habel. *Outback Christmas*. Third edition. Adelaide: Lutheran Publishing House, 1990.
Miles, C. A. *Christmas Customs And Traditions. Their History And Significance*. New York: Dover Publications, 1912/1976.
Mundo, T. "Jesus Christ of the Undocumented". Progressive Theology Web Site. Accessed November 2004.

# Celebration and the Presentness of God

Epiphany 2, 2010
John 2:1-11

Celebration is an important part of religion.
Every time we share in a baptism it is a 'family celebration'.
Same goes for 'most' weddings!

And this morning's gospel theologian, the one we call John,
has told us of one such family celebration... a wedding in Cana.

When we come together to celebrate, be it
a wedding,
a baptism,
a wake,
a graduation,
a community festival
we are affirming a part of life with a joyous 'yes'.

Such is the case with John's story about the wedding at Cana.
But there can be lots of distractions in this story.
And you wouldn't believe the amount of ink
that has been spilt over these distractions!

oo0oo

One such distraction is to read into this a so-called 'miracle'
(even though John doesn't describe anything a miracle)...
So some people get caught,
either because they believe it is, or because they don't.

Another distraction is when some people
worry about the alcoholic content of the wine
and Jesus playing the role of barman—to excess!

While a third distraction is when opponents of same-sex union
call Jesus' attendance at this wedding
his endorsement of marriage as between a man and a woman:
'between Adam & Eve, not Adam & Steve'
to quote both Cardinal George Pell and MP Fred Nile.

But this story is not about any of those issues or concerns.
For I reckon this story is about one simple theme:
Jesus/Yeshua brings life.

As many of Jesus' parables reflect raw, uncensored life,
so here in this created story of a celebration,
John has recast an early Christian story
which has Jesus touching on yet another part of life.

That grace is everywhere. Even in unlikely places.
And any emulation at a literal level is for life.

The love and grace of God are meant to overflow freely for everyone.
Not just in some rarefied New Age sacredness
or fundamentalist Christianity.
Not just in some 'totally' other.

But also lurking in the midst of the grace-full events
of secular human life that ordinary people enjoy.
A spirituality of the secular? Very likely!
For is that not what Incarnation—or more accurately,
'open incarnation'—is?

ooOoo

When I think of the religion of the past
it really concerns me that much of it,
particularly those bits called 'Christianity',
has for too often been seen as a religion of "you shall not."

You shall not drink.
You shall not dance.
You shall not eat meat on Friday.

You shall not enjoy sex.
You shall not associate too closely with those outside your faith.

We draw boundaries around ourselves, and we draw boundaries around God.

- God cannot be found at a wedding party
that includes champagne and dancing, some still say.
- God is not present at birthday parties,
or office Christmas parties, some think.

However, Jesus' actions at the wedding in Cana,
as told to us by John, suggests otherwise.

When the occasions presented themselves Jesus enjoyed life,
celebrated it with family and friends,
embracing community.

Yes, it is very true.
Life is sometimes a bit of rough dirt track
rather than a bitumen superhighway.
And I do not want to be either glib or underestimate
some of the issues we all have to face in our time and day.

Let me offer but one example.
At the World Parliament of Religions held in Melbourne in December 2009,
Sister Joan Chittester was recognised
as 'the real rock star' of the gathering.

Participating in a panel discussion on 'Women and Religion and Poverty'
she made this comment:

> "The first problem, of course, is to distinguish natural poverty from unnatural poverty. The fact that a tsunami might wipe out coastal villages creates a kind of natural poverty that we can only alleviate, not avoid. The fact that women are paid less than men for doing the very same work is unnatural poverty. Of course we can stop that, as we can the exploitation of child labo[u]r and the national greed that underlies it all. But to do all of that, we need to start teaching another version of 'Thou shalt not steal…' which is clearly a religious question.

> "It's impossible to talk about eliminating poverty without talking about the elimination of sexism and the elimination of militarism. Why we seldom hear homilies about those things in Christian churches may be the Christian question of the age" *(Chittister 2009).*

Neither the importance nor the seriousness of that social issue doesn't mean our only response can or should be to avoid life.

Life is good.
Love is good.
Celebrating our joy together is good.

And where life, love, and celebration are present,
it is likely that Creativity God is present as well.

**Notes:**

Chittister, J. "Women and Religion and Poverty" Panel. World Parliament of Religions, Melbourne Australia, 2009.

# A 'Spirituality' on a Journey of Discernment

Epiphany 5, 2009
Mark 1:29-39

In the gospel story we heard from the anonymous storyteller we call Mark, there are four distinct movements.

The healing of Simon Peter's mother in law.
The healing of many people who lived in Capernaum.
A brief solitary prayer.
And the transition to Jesus' public ministry in other towns of Galilee.

From these four movements or life experiences,
Mark is creating a story of a person—the historical Jesus—
who is constantly on a journey, inviting others to re-imagine the world.

The journeying is important.
Indeed, one of the really important phrases from modern scholarship
I resonate with, comes from a bloke called Walter Wink.

In an article called 'The Son of Man', Wink names some of the issues he reckons we need to ponder as we think about the historical Jesus:

- before he was worshipped as God incarnate, how did Jesus struggle to incarnate God?
- before he became identified as the source of all healing, how did he relate to, and how did he teach his disciples to relate to, the healing Source?
- before forgiveness became a function solely of his cross, how did Jesus understand people to have been forgiven?

Wink is saying there is an important difference between the 'historical' Jesus and the 'heavenly' Jesus or Christ of faith.
And if that is not important enough, this phrase:

> "The implications of [this thinking is] profound. We are freed to go on the journey that Jesus chartered, rather than to worship the journey of Jesus... We can take Jesus out of the ghetto of the churches and offer him to anyone looking for a guide to true humanity" *(Wink 2000:177-78).*

Going on the journey rather than worshipping the journey.
Journeying is important.
For individuals and for a congregation.

oo0oo

The story of our journey as a congregation over the past few years has been filled with celebration, with effort, and with frustration.

We've encouraged honesty in our thinking, becoming theologically vulnerable when much of the religious/church life in this city
expects people to suspend their disbelief
for a membership within a community,
or for at least an hour or two each week.

We've opened ourselves in reflection and concern
in the face of international crises such as the Indonesian Tsunami.
As well as to those who have suffered loss through
death,
bush fire,
illnesses, and a changed ecumenical relationship.
Even as we have tried to nurture and care for ourselves.

And we've reached out to the local communities in various ways:
- Community BBQs and Spring Fairs, and
  at the start of the war on Iraq, the Peace Tree in McCulloch St.
- Second-mile Christmas projects,
- The Wellbeing Centre and after some initial decisions taken,
  the independent Centre for Progressive Religious Thought.

When I think of these events, these deeds, these stories and more...
I am both inspired and amazed.
This is a congregation on a journey.

A journey which has taking us to the fore of an important international 'progressive' grassroots movement.
A movement which in its local expression,
explores ministry, religious rituals and community,

in the light of what we now know about the historical Jesus
and the unexplored bits of the Jesus movement traditions.

A journey which tries to make our broader community
a better, more just, and compassionate
'humane' place in which to live.

Even with our rough edges, and I reckon we have a few,
there is much to be thankful for today.

oo0oo

As the children start to return to our Sunday Club program,
and groups start back with planning meetings
and Church Council faces new and challenging decisions,
I would like to think our shared journey over these past nine years
has also been a gathering of strength for your continuing journey, here.

So the challenge this morning, if we would be challenged,
is to begin to wonder and think together
about how we can move on from here
with a spirit of focused courage,
as a community—a people—of a 'progressive' faith.

Because as many of you feel, we are at an important moment of transition.
From a former theology which shaped 'church,
to a newer way of being in community.

Commenting on a similar moment of transition in society in general,
David Tacey, in his book, *The Spirituality Revolution*, says:
"The secular is being besieged by repressed sacred impulses, but religion as it stands cannot relate to these impulses because they speak a different language... and so has marginalised itself from society and life, a tragic situation that has prevented it from showing leadership in the rediscovery of God" *(Tacey 2003:177).*

Tacey's understanding of spirituality seems to be
'either/or'—either spirituality or religion.
A religion you have when you don't feel religious!

Well, if my reading of Tacey is correct, I reckon we need
a more inclusive model of 'spirituality'.
One that offers an important leadership role in religion,
but "beyond the ghetto of the churches" *(Wink 2000:178).*

A model that encourages all of us to explore what it means
to connect to the sacred within, to nature, and to neighbour.
A spirituality of 'progressive' discernment.

That's the important journey we need to continue!
And we can gain courage and strength for **this** journey
by finding in ourselves those powers
that were evident in the sage we call Jesus.

As Walter Wink has said in another important comment:

> "[Jesus] was not God in a mansuit, his every step predetermined from all eternity, but a human being seeking the will of God in the everyday decisions that shape life [and] living..." *(Wink 2000:178).*

We could do no better than to share in that same journey
and in that same discernment, in our own time and place. Now.

The challenge is to shed all the accumulated baggage, while
not slipping backwards into some ho-hum, all-purpose 'middle',
symbolised by a car's rear-view mirror!

For this journey to continue we will need
a sense of expectancy,
a glimpse of future possibilities,
a vivid imagination—and plenty of niche courage!

For Creativity God's creation in this place is not done.

**Notes:**

Tacey, D. *The Spirituality Revolution. The EmergenceOof Contemporary Spirituality*. Sydney: HarperCollins, 2003.
Wink, W. "The Son of Man" in R. W. Funk (ed). *The Once And Future Jesus*. Santa Rosa: Polebridge Press, 2000.

# Snorting Indignation while Boundaries are Pushed

Epiphany 6, 2009
Mark 1:40-45

It seems the most common area of dispute between neighbours
is not loud music,
or late night parties,
or even dogs that poop on one's nature strip.

The most common area of dispute is the boundary fence.
Its colour.
Its material.
Its cost.
Its position.

This morning's story of the healing of a so-called 'leper'
or 'unclean' one, by the anonymous storyteller we call Mark,
is also about boundaries.

Because the religion in which Jesus grew up—noble, ethical, admirable—
had arrived at a place where it apparently drew such strict boundaries,
most people were on the other side of them.

And taking seriously the context of this particular story,
anyone with a noticeable disfigurement or abnormality,
whatever that may be,
was bound under the 'outsiders' religious rule of the day
to announce his or her coming, when approaching another.

To carry, as it were, his or her own boundary.
"Unclean, unclean" the 'leper' probably said, as he approached
the Jewish sage, Jesus.

Now traditionally there has been much said about the so-called purity
Laws, and Christian interpretations given the 686 commandments
have not always been helpful.

Such interpretations usually paint all Jews of Jesus' time
as the bad blokes, and Jesus as the good bloke.
Which is not only unfair, and at times untrue,
it is also dangerous *(Levine 2006:28-29).*

Needless to say, I am not going to play that game!
But what I will say is it appears some level of 'boundaries' did help Israel
maintain her identity amid all the other
cultures and religions of the day.

Which of course, is nothing new. Either then. Or now.
We in Australia know all about boundaries.
In the past it was called 'The White Australia Policy'!

Listen to Liberal politician Billy Snedden back in 1969 when,
as Minister for Immigration, he said in parliamentary debate:

> "We must have a single culture—if immigrants implied multiculture activities within Australian society, then it was not the type Australia wanted. I am quite determined we should have a monoculture, with everyone living in the same way, understanding each other, and sharing the same aspirations. We don't want pluralism" *(Galvin & West 1988:63).*

oo0oo

So let me share with you a couple of things about this story
by the anonymous storyteller we call Mark.

The first is... Jesus/Yeshua did not cure this leper of Hansen's disease,
the ailment known to modern medicine as leprosy.

In biblical times the term leprosy embraced
a wide range of disorders, including
rashes,
acne,
eczema
and other forms of dermatitis.

Leprosy was sometimes regarded as divine punishment for sin,
but it was not considered an incurable disease.
    That's the first thing.

The second is... our storyteller says a person,
regarded by all as 'unclean', approaches Jesus.
    And Jesus/Yeshua makes a response.
    But what was that response.

Some ancient manuscripts use a word to mean "having pity".
Other manuscripts use a word to mean "being angry".

Those who are members of the *Jesus Seminar* offer this translation:

> "Although Jesus was indignant, he stretched out his hand, touched him, and says to him, 'Okay—you're clean!'" *(Funk & Hoover 1993:43)*

The *Inclusive Text* which we heard this morning takes a different approach:

> "Moved with pity, Jesus stretched out his hand and touched him, and said to him, 'I do choose. Be made clean!'"

Most translations, it seems, have gone with
the emotion of "pity" or "compassion".
    I can see where both emotions, 'compassion' or 'anger',
    would have been appropriate.

Jesus shows compassion to a person forced to live
on the edges or boundaries of society.

Jesus shows a "snort of anger" *(Cairns 2004:24)* with a system
that forces such people into that situation.

Ched Myers, in his challenging commentary on Mark
called *Binding the Strong Man*, suggests:
    "The cleansed leper's task is not to publicise a miracle but to help
    confront an ideological system..." *(Myers 2008)*.

An ideological system which draws boundaries between
    the acceptable and the unacceptable,
    the 'clean' and the 'unclean'.

But as another commentator has warned:

Be careful when you draw lines. Whenever you draw a line which helps to tell you who is in and who is out of God's people, remember, Jesus is always on the other side of the line!

oo0oo

Jesus' vision of the 'God realm' or 'God empire'
was one of inclusive wholeness.
So, in this story by Mark
it restores people's humanity and life,
it invites people to grasp new opportunities to rejoin the community,
it re-imagines the world.
That is, Jesus' actions "decontaminated the leper" *(Loader 2006).*

I reckon we miss all of that if we insist this story
is about a supernatural curing
that depends on the intervention of God...

Similarly, the stories that tell of Jesus' open and inclusive table.
We will miss their radical nature if we only imagine these meals
as casual social acts, as they can be in our modern world.

Back then, the meal or table fellowship was an embodiment
of a social vision of
hierarchies,
differences,
distinctions, and
discriminations.

But the 'open' meal practice of Jesus/Yeshua became a cultural protest.
It challenged the ethos and politics of holiness
which had led to a closed table fellowship.

It embodied an alternative vision of an inclusive community.
It reflected the compassion of God
and the absolute equality of people.

And this vision and this practise clashed fundamentally
with the basic values of ancient Mediterranean society.
Especially where the difference between the rich and the working poor
was often reduced to a mutual competition for status and resources.

oo0oo

The God of Jesus/Yeshua, according to storyteller Mark, is a God
of graciousness and goodness and a booster of self esteem,
who accepts everyone and brings about
justice and well-being for everyone... without exception.

That's worth celebrating.
And where it is denied, that's worth getting angry about!

**Notes:**


Cairns, I. J. *Mark Of A Non-realist. A Contemporary Reading Of The Second Gospel.* Masterton: Fraser Books, 2004.

Funk, R. W. & R. W. Hoover. (ed) *The Five Gospels. The Search For The Authentic Words Of Jesus.* New York: Macmillan Press, 1993.

Galvin, M.; P. West. *A Changing Australia. Themes And Case Studies.* Marrickville.:Harcourt Brace Jovanovich Group, 1988.

*Inclusive Readings. Year B.* Brisbane: Inclusive Language Project. In private circulation, 2005.

Loader, W. "Lectionary Resources". http://wwwstaff.murdoch.edu.au/~loader/lectionaryindex.html Accessed 2006.

Levine, A-J. *The Misunderstood Jew. The Church And The Scandal Of The Jewish Jesus.* New York: HarperOne, 2006.

Myers, C. *Binding The Strong Man. A Political Reading Of Mark's Story Of Jesus.* Special edition. Maryknoll: Orbis Books, 2008.

# Artisan Jesus and the Re-Imagined Kin-dom

Epiphany 7, 2011
Matthew 5:38-48

Let me share with you a couple of observations
as we begin to unpack the sayings of Matthew's Jesus/Yeshua
on 'turn the other cheek',
'go an extra way', and
'love enemies'.

For these sayings are not only part of some biblical stories,
they also come down to us in popular culture.

oo0oo

My first observation and introduction.
Most 'progressive religion' people would recognise the name of Marcus Borg.
He is an author of several books, a Fellow of the Jesus Seminar, and
recognised as one of the scholars within
the world-wide 'progressive Christianity' movement.

In his dialogue with conservative evangelical scholar Tom Wright,
Borg tells a story about teaching an introductory-level course
on the Bible at Oregon State University…
A course he taught for more than 25 years.

In that class he could nearly always predict
that around 20% of those enrolled

> "[would] be very conservative in their attitude toward the Bible, either from their upbringing or because they are recent converts to conservative forms of college Christianity" *(Borg 1999:238).*

So each year he would introduce the course stating it would be taught
from the "academic discipline of biblical scholarship"
which emphasises that

> "it does not see the Bible as divine in origin but as human, namely, as the product of two ancient communities… As

such, the Bible tells us not how God sees things, but how those two ancient communities saw things" *(Borg 1999:239).*

As would happen, during the first couple of weeks
there usually was a fair amount of squabbling between Borg
"and the more bold and articulate of the conservative students" *(Borg 1999:239).*

But during the mid-1990s a very bright Muslim student,
taking the course, observed this 'squabbling', and said to Borg:
"I think I understand what's going on here. You're saying the Bible is like a lens through which we see God, and they're saying that it's important to believe in the lens" *(Borg 1999:239).*

Borg agreed:
"Yeah, that's what I'm saying... [B]eing a Christian... is not about believing in the Bible or the gospels or Christian teachings about Jesus, but about a relationship to the One whom we see through the lens of the Christian tradition as a whole" *(Borg 1999:239).*

Now to my second observation and introduction.
Arthur Dewey is an author, a radio commentator on religion,
a progressive theologian, and like Borg,
a Fellow of the Jesus Seminar.

In one of his many articles he explores the possibility of
viewing Jesus through the 'lens', to use the Muslim student's image,
of a peasant artisan or craftsman.

Why this particular 'lens'?.
Dewey reckons this could help us work out what Jesus was about.
He writes:
"It appreciates the texture of his imagination. How did Jesus craft his words? What did he envision as he worked? How did his words invite his listeners into his vision...What can we make of those words? *(Dewey 2002:73).*

So, how does he suggest Jesus/Yeshua went about crafting his words?

Dewey goes on:

> "Working in wood or stone demands envisioning 'what is there within' the material… He 'sees' what is 'there' and works painstakingly toward it. The task is to see a vision and to use the 'grain' in seeking to realize that vision *(Dewey 2002:74)*.

And then this comparison:

> "The same is true for an artisan in words…The storyteller searches for the words to communicate a vision that generates, sustains, and moves the words forward. The historical Jesus was not only a craftsman but an artisan of words" *(Dewey 2002:74)*.

A lens.
A craftsman.
An artisan.

Suggestions by two scholars—Borg and Dewey—whose invitations to us
are to grapple and struggle with these sayings
as did the early Christian communities.
Because as we are finding out more and more these days,
there was no unity and certainty of meaning at the beginning.

So let's rub these suggestions together, in stereo if you like,
with the sayings from Matthew's Jesus, about
'turn the cheek', 'go an extra way' and 'love enemies'.

What might we get from these words.

oo0oo

As modern members of the human race we are facing some major problems:

- energy use, ecology and the environment,
- politics, poverty, war, just to mention a few.

Not only do these problems face us in a universal sense,
they can also be framed by one or two other equally big questions:

(i) What does it mean to be human? And how did we come to be the way
we are?
(ii) What is our destiny? And what is the path to that destiny?

Now I want to suggest these latter questions are suitable imaginative lenses for us to look at these sayings.

As I also want to speculate that similar questions may have been the imaginative lenses through which the historical Jesus looked,
as folk gathered at meals or beside a lake,
to listen to this sage.

So what might artisan Jesus/Yeshua have 'seen…
what is there within' his audience?
I offer these suggestions I have gleaned along the way
and invite you to ponder them some more.

For they:
(i) dispute the conventional wisdom that says one's primary concern should be for those within our own social group or clan or family or nationality;
(ii) admit there is a degree of alienation in society, be it towards Muslims, gays and lesbians, or so-called illegal boat people/immigrants— whom we or they often turn into 'the enemy', and
(iii) challenge us all to reshape our social categories, especially those of others, formed by our fears and rumours and innuendo.

And what might be the 'grain' to realise this required
re-imagining or new vision?
Or indeed the lens of the Christian tradition as a whole?
Arthur Dewey suggests:

> "…can you imagine acting differently towards those outside the circle of your people? …not only to reimagine [your] response but also to offer [your] oppressor a chance for a more [humane] reply" *(Dewey 2002:80).*

Challenges, I suggest, which are likely to go to the core of
what it means to be human!

oo0oo

When we rub these sayings together we get a stereo response.
At least that's what I reckon the historical Jesus was suggesting in these saying.
Take some space to re-imagine your so-called 'natural' response.
Give the other party/person space to act more humanely.

But, as we know and as the historical Jesus knew, I reckon,
this crafted vision can only come true
when our social consciences are reconstructed
responsibly, creatively, and with humility.

Or to use some 21st century language:
"active listening entails [a] continued artistic response… a subtle crafting of the Kingdom" *(Dewey 2002:86).*

I invite your active pondering!

**Notes:**

Borg, M. J. 'A vision of the Christian life' in M. J. Borg & N. T Wright. *The Meaning Of Jesus. Two Visions.* New York: HarperSanFrancisco, 1999.
Dewey, A. J. 'Jesus as a peasant artisan' in R. W. Hoover (ed) *Profiles Of Jesus.* Santa Rosa: Polebridge Press, 2002.

# The Temptation to Do Good?

Lent 1, 2002
Matthew 4:1-11

What an appropriate outback story in this the Year of the Outback!
Jesus is led into the outback, into the desert.
No McDonald's just around the corner.
No Toyota 4-wheel drive to get him through the flooded creeks.
No fleecy lined sleeping bag or Sundowner tent
to keep out the wind, the flies, and the dust storms.

He must live off the land and his own wits to survive.
If they were to make a TV series about it,
they would probably be tempted to call it 'Survivor'!

And during that experience, so the story goes, Jesus is tested.
He is urged to perform miracles and the like
in order that good events would come to pass.

Yes, tested, tempted, to do... good!

Now I suspect most of us are not used to that kind of thinking about 'temptations'.
We're used to thinking of temptations as something bad.
Usually morally 'bad', and connected with
a member of the opposite gender!

Yet the options that were waved under Jesus' nose, says Matthew,
are all based on three popular views of the Messiah, current at that time:
caregiver,
wonder worker, and
source of power.

And they all would result in 'good', as opposed to bad or evil.
The hungry would be fed.
People would be led back to God.
The countries of the world would experience peace and justice
under God's imperial rule.

Fair enough.
Sounds a lot like what we say every week in this congregation...
in the words in the spirit of The '*Abba*' Prayer.

Yet this still doesn't ring totally true.
So what is it that's missing?
Maybe we should take a look at this story from another direction.

Let me offer a personal observation or two.

oo0oo

I find it particularly interesting that this week, this Lent, in this city,
our national Parliament began its new Session
faced with a protest against the government's treatment
of asylum seekers—in the desert areas of Australia.

Each party also began this Session with a 'wilderness' experience of its own,
even if it was in the luxury of Parliament House,
seeking to define its 'vocational' focus for the next few months.

Months, when some of the most important and inflammatory issues
are likely to return to the political and Australian agenda.

Likewise, in Matthew's 'wilderness' story, the focus of Jesus' testing
is vocational rather than a lesson about private morality.

Indeed, according to the scholars of the *Jesus Seminar*,
they are a symbolic testing of the kind
not uncommon in the stories of the lives of great heroes
in the ancient world.

Take time out to face who you are and what is your calling!
Face up to the alternatives!

In Lent, in particular, we are reminded of the importance
of doing so for ourselves. This is something
not just for heroes or political parties.

So what agenda might drive us?

The anonymous storyteller we call Matthew
tells a Jesus hero story about options and conflict
and the inmost workings of Jesus' mind.

And the major focus of the story is on Jesus saying 'no' to certain models.
Models which not only might have been options for Jesus himself,
but also could have been models for later Christians
seeking to be at mission in the way of Jesus
such as Matthew's own small community.

You are familiar with those options.
One option offered by 'the hinderer' is to gain followers
through stunts or miracles.
A common option then and now, I'm afraid.

Another is to take the military option: achieve dominion by force.
While yet another could be to join the revolutionary movements of the day.

West Australian theologian William (Bill) Loader reminds us:

> "Such traditions and expectations colour the gospel accounts of Jesus' ministry. We can be sure that many would have listened to the fantasy of Jesus' great trial with such things in mind" *(Loader 2002).*

All these options, Matthew takes from stories that were circulating
in the communities about this itinerant preacher-sage.
Yet with a sense of real concern,
he offers them as a teaching opportunity to his group.

Teaching such as:

• there will always be false gods—the will to power, materialism, and a spirituality of the sensational—and saying 'no' to these other gods
will require open and honest discerning of
what it is that Creativity God is about in the world.

ooOoo

There are plenty of spirituality's on offer today to each and every one of us. Some of them are so-called secular—from within various political movements. Some are religious—including from within Christianity.

Others get plenty of air time on late night talk-back radio programs or display space at conventions and special events.
Which is the way to go? That can be the $64 question, can't it!

Let me again offer some personal observations.

One way to go, is to retain a sense of critical theological reflection about what shapes our beliefs and church life.

Because ultimately what shapes our beliefs,
especially our Christian life, depends on what
we understand G-o-d or the Sacred to be.

Belief in a God which is external, supernatural and invasive,
to borrow some thoughts from (Bishop) Jack Spong,
is an entirely different understanding of God, 'named'
as presence, creativity, sacred, and mysterious.

Likewise, I am convinced we need to hear Matthew's story
of the conflict between Jesus/Yeshua and 'the hinderer',
as a story about Jesus seeking to discover
his own sense of self and/or vocation.
And not some pious statement about private morality,
often used to batter others around the head with.

But of sensing both what God/the Sacred is doing in human life
and discerning how he, Jesus/Yeshua, and other people
should creatively and compassionately and inclusively, respond.

And sometimes that meant for Jesus/Yeshua,
as it will so often mean for us,
making a choice and saying a surprising 'no'
to the temptation to do good.

**Notes:**

Loader, W. "First Thoughts on Gospel Passages from the Lectionary".
http://wwwstaff.murdoch.edu.au/~loader/lectionaryindex.html
Accessed February 2002.

# Truth... and Being a Blessing or a Curse

Lent 4, 2008
John 9:1, 6-9, 13-17, 33-34

Let me share with you three short story cameos.

• The first cameo comes from a friend in Melbourne who got it from the web.
I know the name of the author but for reasons
which I feel you will readily twig to later, I will not disclose.
But I can say he is a Jesuit priest.

[In September 2004], I spoke to some 2,000 students during their annual lecture at a Baptist college in Pennsylvania.
After a short prayer service for peace centred on the Beatitudes,
I took the stage and got right to the point.
'Now let me get this straight,' I said. 'Jesus says, Blessed are the peace makers, which means he does not say, Blessed are the war makers, which means, the war makers are not blessed, which means war makers are cursed, which means, if you want to follow the non-violent Jesus you have to work for peace, which means, we all have to resist this horrific, evil war on the people of Iraq.'

With that, the place exploded, and 500 students stormed out.
The rest of them started chanting, 'Bush! Bush! Bush!'
So much for my speech.
Not to mention the Beatitudes.

• A second cameo.
It comes from a communications resource book by Don Fabun
which I have used in seminars in days long past.
It is an ancient Hindu story of six blind people and an elephant.

Six blind people came upon an elephant.

The first one touched the elephant's side
And at once began to bawl:
'God bless me! The elephant is very like a wall'.

The second one felt the tusk.
'To me it's very clear, the elephant is very like a spear'.

The third one grabbed the elephant's ear and said:
'Deny the fact if you can, but an elephant is very like a fan'.

The one who had hold of the trunk boldly spake:
'You fool! The elephant is very like a long, thick snake!'

The fifth one, who had bumped into a leg, said:
'You're all crazy! I have a firm hold on this elephant,
and it is very like a tree'.

And from behind,
the one who had grabbed the tail, called out:
'It's not a large thing at all, you dope.
Indeed it is very like a small, stiff rope!'

And so these folk disputed loud and long,
each in their own opinion, exceeding stiff and strong.
Though each was partly in the right.
They all were in the wrong!

• The third cameo.
One day the devil and one of his little helpers,
were sitting on a cloud looking down at the humans below,
    when they saw a man walking down a road
    who stopped, picked up something from the road,
    put it in his pocket and walked on.

"What did he find?" asked the devil's helper.
"A piece of the truth," chuckled the devil.

"A piece of the truth? Don't you want to stop him?"

"Stop him? Oh no," said the devil. It's only a tiny piece of truth.
Before long, he'll turn it into an orthodoxy.
    And then he'll be doing my work!" *(Bausch 1998)*

oo0oo

John, our anonymous biblical storyteller for today,
really knows his craft.
He weaves one story in and around another story.

The story of a disabled person—a blind man,
who begins to grasp some of the new possibilities
of Jesus' re-imagined world.
And starts to act upon them.

And a second story of what some religious leaders did
when they too began to sense some of the implications
of this re-imagined world.
And start to act upon their fears.

But all is not as clear as that!
To begin with, it's a story woven around another story where the subject matter,
I want to suggest, isn't about healing or curing
but about how big or small are our claims of 'truth'
and how we frame those claims.

So let me tease out some of this suggestion just a little.

oo0oo

Rumour has it, John the storyteller wasn't that keen
on many of the Jewish leaders of his day.

Indeed, I reckon it is more than a rumour.
At times—many times—this storyteller is quite 'anti-Jewish'.
But that doesn't always come out in the traditional
Christian interpretations of John's stories.

Take today's story again.

Several biblical scholars, including some Australian biblical scholars,
advance the view it is highly likely that by the time John was writing,
his small community (the so-called reformers)
had been excommunicated from main stream Judaism
(the so-called orthodox).

That one group was seen to be 'open'. The other group was seen to be 'closed'.
That one group was seen as 'inclusive'. The other group was seen as 'obsessive'.
That one group advocated a broader based 'truth'. The other group
claimed a narrower based 'truth'.

John's language is much more strident than what I have just said.
He has Jewish Jesus say of the Jews, for instance:
'You are from your father the devil, and you choose to do your father's desires. He was a murderer… he lies…' *(John 8:44, NRSV).*

Would such a similar statement if levelled at us, go down well in this place?
I would think not!
I think we would have a membership problem on our hands!

Jewish New Testament scholar Amy-Jill Levine,
who is our mentor during this year's Lenten season, says:
"Despite the lack of evidence that there was an empire-wide expulsion of Christians from synagogues or that Jews around 90 were cursing Christians… the Pontifical Biblical Commission [for example] goes so far as to suggest that Jews were not only expelling Christ-confessors but also murdering them" *(Levine 2006:108).*

She goes on:
"The picture this description presents is of nasty Jews who persecute innocent Christians for loving God, loving neighbor, and worshiping the Christ" *(Levine 2006:108).*

John has, I reckon, been swamped by dangerous propaganda,
the effects of which, have been felt as anti-Judaism
and anti-Semitic around the world,
and even fuelled a world war or two!

Such rigidity as expressed by John, must be denounced.
And denounced by progressive Christian theology.

Because such rigidity can lead to some being
"willing to fight or even kill for the[ir] truth, [that] they don't realize... they are among [truth's] greatest enemies—and that they make the devil laugh with glee at his newest disciples" *(Loehr 2008).*

So, what about the suggestion that John's story
is about 'truth' rather than 'healing'?
I have difficulty with accepting the notion
that you allow one group to define 'truth' for someone else.

As I was reminded again by another Davidson Loehr comment:
"when the only tool you own is a hammer, everything looks like a nail. It... takes more and better tools to serve either truth or life"
*(Loehr 2008).*

So perhaps we can start by acknowledging that none of us
will ever have all the 'truth'.
We are all, if you like, that person who picked up
a 'truthlet'—who picked up just a tiny piece of truth.

Thus the 'truth' journey we could encourage for ourselves, is:
- Has what we've been following, made us a curse or a blessing to others.
- Has what we've become, increased or decreased
the amount of understanding and compassion in the world.

The Bible is capable of taking on innumerable interpretations.
Critical scholarly work can be helpful in eliminating
some of the negative interpretations.

Yet some of the so-called 'positive' interpretations
can also have serious negative effects.

We live in a multicultural, multi-faith society.
And often Paul's so-called 'inclusive' proclamation that:
There is no longer Jew or Greek, no longer slave or free, no longer male or female... in Christ Jesus *(Galatians 3:28, NRSV)* is held up as 'good news' for all.

"But", says Amy-Jill Levine again:
"to state that in the ideal world... 'there is no longer Jew or Greek' sounds like an erasure of Jewish (and Greek) identity. Christian universalism thus entails the erasure of anything distinctly Jewish. Those who seek to promote multiculturalism might wish to rephrase Paul's language to celebrate 'both Jew and Greek, both male and female, and all, who should be free"
*(Levine 2006:114).*

Similar comments can also be said
of parts of the synagogue liturgy and language.

That they can sound 'anti-Christian' to Christian ears.

I hope these thoughts might be worth pondering some more
as we continue during Lent,
to travel on the journey
that Jesus/Yeshua first chartered.

**Notes:**


Bausch, W. *A World Of Stories For Preachers And Teachers*. Mystic: Twenty-Third Publications, 1998.

Fabun, D. *Communications. The Transfer Of Meaning*. Beverley Hills: Glencoe Press, 1968.

Levine, A-J. *The Misunderstood Jew. The Church And The Scandal Of The Jewish Jesus*. New York: HarperOne, 2006.

Loehr, D. "A Sermon". First UU Austin Church Web site. http://austinuu.org/ Accessed 2008.

*Holy Bible NRSV*. Nashville: Thomas Nelson Publishers, 1989.

# The Palm Sunday Challenge to Set Jesus Free

Palm Sunday, 2008
Matthew 21:1-4, 6-11

It was the first day of the last week of life for Jesus of Nazareth.
According to storyteller Matthew Jesus had arrived
in Bethphage, at the Mount of Olives,
a short walk from Jerusalem.

A couple of days later he indicated he was joining the procession of people making their way into Jerusalem
to celebrate the feast of freedom—the feast of the Passover.
And our storyteller says: there was a reaction.

Australian New Testament theologian William (Bill) Loader, says we shouldn't picture this entry as an historical event

"... in which the whole of Jerusalem lined the streets, thronging the new Messiah. An actual entry with some shouts of praise doubtless occurred but would have been sufficiently lost in the Passover crowds as not to warrant the military's attention, who would have been swift to put an end to what could have seemed like a potential disturbance. Whatever the event, it became highly symbolic," *(Loader 2002).*

Loader continues with the suggestion that Jesus/Yeshua
was not entering a foreign city,
nor entering the city of 'the Jews'.
He was a Jew.
He was entering the city which symbolised in his faith
and his scriptures, God's promise to Israel.

Marcus Borg and John Crossan, in their book *The Last Week*, also suggest:

"Jerusalem was not just any city. By the first century, it had been the center of the sacred geography of the Jewish people for a millennium. And ever since, it has been central to the sacred

imagination of both Jews and Christians" *(Borg & Crossan 2006:5).*
Neither was Jesus' entry designed as a great PR opportunity
because of the larger than usual number of people
in Jerusalem during Passover.

Rather his entry—one of two to take place—was an action which
in itself is full of 'parable' meaning.
For it was an action—even a desperate confronting action—
which had as its focus a desire for, a hope for, change.

Perhaps that is why the anonymous storyteller we call Matthew
has the crowd remembering the prophets
and recognising Jesus as 'the prophet from Nazareth'.
The bringer of change and wholeness and healing.

oo0oo

To confront one's own faith and its traditions in a call for change,
can be a very painful experience.
Because it means challenging existing structures of authority.

So I guess you will not be surprised to hear me say
that those who have inspired and challenged me theologically,
have usually been those who have confronted
rather than supported the orthodox traditions of the faith.

That is what I understand is the 'liberal' or 'progressive' tradition
within the church… or 'against the stream' as one of my mentors,
Henry Nelson Wieman, puts it.

Those who have inspired and challenged me have included:
Wieman (just mentioned), John A. T. Robinson, Lloyd Geering,
Sallie McFague, John Shelby Spong, Brandon Scott, Nigel Leaves, and
Stephen Patterson.
Some of you will recognise some of those names.

Yet coupled with these theologians,
and sometimes standing over against them,
there has been for me a parallel interest in

what is called 'Celtic spirituality':

- the sense of the presentness of God within the universe;
- the sense of the presentness of God in the everyday, the ordinary;
- the sense of the presentness of God as Creativity.

So when I read and hear the Palm Sunday story, especially this year from Matthew, and take on board the suggestion that this story
does not gain its authenticity from any triumphalist interpretation,
but instead is a passionate parable about a call for change,
then as the bloke used to say on the TV: I'm excited!

But... and yes there is a 'but'.
I also admit to being concerned about the current state of the church,
and the at times lack of courage for theological change.

Concerned, because I agree with many of the critics who claim:
it is not hard to see that a Christian church

- which seems to reward fundamentalism,
- is concerned with the spiritual to the exclusion of the material,
- and is shackled to ineffable dullness…

creates so many 'exiles'.

So I gain some comfort from the likes of Bishop Jack Spong
when he writes:

> "Religion... is not an activity designed to control behaviour, to reward virtue, and to punish vice. Religion is, rather, a human attempt to process the God experience, which breaks forth from our own depths and wells up constantly within us" *(Spong 1998:225).*

oo0oo

It was Palm Sunday... the first day of the last week of life
for Jesus of Nazareth.
Jesus had (once again?) come home
to the place of his faith and his scriptures.

This Palm Sunday we have the advantage of 2000+ years
of scholarly insight behind us, especially in the areas of
the origins and history of the Christian tradition.

But sadly those in the church who love 'doctrine' and 'orthodoxy'
have not always welcomed those who offer challenging 'scholarship'.
An invisible wall of silence has often prevented this
'new scholarship' from entering the faith and life of the churches.

With the result that in many mainline churches,
bureaucrats and clergy have become frozen by fear:
fear of shrinking numbers,
fear of a lack of financial resources,
fear of the world,
fear of disturbing a slumbering 'peace'.

But scholarship does matter.
And as the Jesus Seminar Robert (Bob) Funk often stressed:
(i) biblical scholars have an ethical responsibility to speak not just privately but publicly, and not just obscurely but clearly, and
(ii) there is a whole lay constituency—inside and outside the church—ready, willing, and able to join in that public discourse.

So this Palm Sunday I invite you to risk the way of sound scholarship.
Where genuine curiosity and inquiry is welcomed.
Where asking deep questions is more important
than running after easy answers.

And to "set Jesus free" as Funk suggests *(Funk 1996:21)*, and to
"liberate Jesus from the scriptural and creedal and experiential prisons in which we have incarcerated him" *(Funk 1996:300)*.

Then maybe his going to Jerusalem will have been worth it!

**Notes:**


Borg, M. & J D Crossan. *The Last Week. A Day-by-Day Account Of Jesus's Final Week In Jerusalem*. New York: HarperSanFrancisco, 2006.

Funk, R. W. *Honest To Jesus. Jesus For A New Millennium*. New York: HarperSanFrancisco, 1996.

Loader, W. "First Thoughts on Gospel Passages from the Lectionary". http://wwwstaff.murdoch.edu.au/~loader/lectionaryindex.html Accessed 2005.

Spong, J. S. *Why Christianity Must Change Or Die. A Bishop Speaks To Believers In Exile*. New York: HarperSanFrancisco, 1998.

# Good Friday: Not Being Defeated by Violence

Good Friday, 2011
John 18:1 to 19:42

In the routine hell of Auschwitz, towards the end of July 1941,
ten men were lined up to be starved to death
    in the dreaded underground bunker
    as a reprisal for an escape attempt.

One of them cried out,
    "My wife, my children, what will become of them?"

A somewhat rhetorical question in the conditions of that time,
and in that place of four million executions.

A thin, battered man, prisoner 16670, stepped forward,
and offered to die in the place of his fellow prisoner.

The second surprise in that brutal place was that his offer was accepted.
So it happened that this 47 year old Catholic priest
    was put down into the starvation bunker with the other nine.

To all reports, strange things happened in the next two weeks:
    hymns,
    expressions of forgiveness,
    prayers,
    prisoners singing as they died.

When they came to finish off No. 16670 with an injection of phenol,
for he was the last to die, they found him propped up against the wall
with a joyful smile on his face.

Forty-one years later Maximilian Kolbe was canonised.
Not merely for the way he died, but for the way he lived, months before,
as a source of extraordinary hope and strength
    for his fellow-sufferers in that hell.

The man he saved was present at his canonisation *(Bausch 1998).*

oo0oo

Jesus died because he was publicly and brutally executed.
He certainly did not want to die...

Our tradition says with loud cries and tears, he prayed to the One
whom others claimed could have saved him from death.
He died as a result of his passionate, imaginative living.
He died as a result of a decision not to deviate from the
God-Self-Neighbour relationship he continually lived.

It is difficult today to have a sense of the utter obscenity
and degradation attached to crucifixion.
Now, the sign of the cross has become a routine liturgical gesture
as well as a fashion statement. It is 'in' to wear one.

Then, it was an obscene thing,
not to be mentioned in the hearing of a Roman.

As a form of execution, it was the ultimate deterrent
for the subversive and the slave.
The ultimate way of dealing with anyone
judged to be a threat to the sacred order.

In the name of all the gods of that order Jesus was condemned.
What Jesus said and did and stood for... collided with Roman imperial religion.
He was killed by the Roman authority, who could not accept
the countercultural effect of his teaching and example:

"loving self, neighbor and enemy through the passive resistance of
turning a second cheek to the smiter of the first, of giving up
shirt as well as coat when need demanded, of swearing off grudges
as often as it took and a pact among people to treat each other
with mutual consideration" *(Cook 2011).*

All these tore open the social and religious fabric of his time.
This new cloth could not be sewn onto an old garment.
This new wine could not be kept in the old wineskins.
Either that social and religious order, or Jesus/Yeshua, had to go.

He was executed because what he did and said
was so deeply subversive of the politico-religious order of his day.
Justice had indeed been done!

oo0oo

Some say the season of Lent calls us to 'reflection'. Others say, 'repentance'.
With yet others I want to claim the day called Good Friday
calls us to 'opposition'.
To stand in solidarity with others.
To stand against even the church where its solidarity has been
with the Empire rather than with the oppressed.

The memory of Jesus/Yeshua is
dangerous,
subversive,
death-threatening,
life-affirming,
bursting with hope,
and mindful of evil.

Christianity that is true to the life of the one we call Jesus
"tells his death as the story of resistance to the Roman Empire, not as the story of how the Empire enacted God's will... The gospels constructed an innovative strategy to resist crucifixion. They rejected the terror that crucifixion instilled and told the story another way, against the grain of historical fact and with the grain of love and resistance" *(Brock 2008).*

Rita Brock, in her powerful book *Saving Paradise*,
co-authored with Rebecca Parker, goes further:
"Their telling affirmed divine presence in human flesh, in Jesus who showed them how to live, *before* he died, and revealed love stronger than terror, torture, or death" *(Brock 2008).*

If Good Friday is to mean anything in our time and our place
"we must break [the] silence whenever violence is used to shame, instill fear, fragment human community, or suppress our work for economic justice, health care, and peace" *(Brock 2008).*

Traditional theology has taught us:
'Jesus died so we might live'.
It suggests the torture and murder lamented this Friday is "good."

Progressive theology teaches:
Christians who ground their power in divine love mourn on Friday, keep vigil until dawn on Sunday, and say with joy,
Jesus *lived* so that all creation might live.

**Notes:**

Bausch, W. J. *A World Of Stories For Preachers And Teachers*. Mystic: Twenty-Third Publications, 1998.
Brock, R. & R Parker. *Saving Paradise: How Christianity Traded Love Of This World For Crucifixion And Empire***.** Boston: Beacon Press, 2008.
Cook, H. T. "Responsible Self-Determination". http://www.harrytcook.com/ Accessed April 2011.

# Life Invites Us to Be Startled by Easter, Not Scared by It

Easter Day B, 2009
Mark 16:1-8

Two single autumn leaves are on an otherwise barren tree branch.
One leaf says to the other:
    Say, why do we have to fall from the tree around Easter time
    in Canberra and die, anyway?

The other leaf begins to expound:
    Well, the way I understand it, when autumn comes,
    changes begin to occur in the cells where our stem is attached to the branch…
    and the vessels which supply us with nourishment become plugged
    with gums causing us to wither and fall from the tree.

The first leaf responds:
    That isn't going to happen to me.
    I know the answer.
    I exercise!

oo0oo

When it comes to celebrating Easter, we 21st century Australians
do so in several ways.
    We celebrate it as a holiday.
    We usually celebrate it by 'going away'.
    We always celebrate it by eating... 'hot cross buns', smoked cod
    and chocolate Easter eggs.
And we, the minority that is, sometimes celebrate it by going to church.

Today is Easter Day 2009. Tradition has it as the most
important day in the life of the church.
    For it is the day when we hear again
        not just the stories of an ending
        but the stories of new beginnings.

So what can be said on this day, Easter 2009,
that hasn't already been said before?
Usually not much, because we claim we know the answer!

But maybe there can be just enough said so we are reminded
that out of evil can come good,
and that out of grief there can come new strength, new beginnings.

oo0oo

Much ink and blood, sweat and tears, have been spilt
over 'what is' and 'what is not' considered to be the real Easter story.
And of course, what is meant by 'resurrection'.

And that includes all the problematic stuff argued by a bloke we call Paul!
And the thousands of trees chopped down in the name of an 'empty tomb'!
And whether or not the 'resurrection' was a 'resuscitated body'
or an event in the lives of the disciples!

All this, while also noting that all the biblical stories are different, and
none of the storytellers provide an unambiguous,
totally convincing account!

Today's anonymous gospel storyteller is a bloke we call Mark.
His take on things was an early comment.
And theologically, he seems to be put off by

> "postmortem appearance stories, and steered clear of them altogether… But [his] empty tomb story would have appealed more widely to readers in the Jewish and Hellenistic world, who would have heard similar stories told of heroes who had been rescued from dire straits and translated directly to heaven to live safely with the gods" *(Patterson 2004:114).*

Indeed, if we only stay with the biblical stories, no one
is convinced by the 'empty tomb'. So why should we try to be?

Now I know some of you have heard all this,
and probably more, before.
From me. And from others.
Which, along with all the traditional Christian art you have ever

seen about the resurrection, and by the way, needs to be
excised from you imagination *(Scott 2008: 1),*
always makes sermons on Easter morning difficult to preach.

So perhaps at some risk let me offer a few of my thoughts.
Maybe they will gel with some of yours.
Maybe they will conflict with yours.

But they are mine, learned over time.

And in the company of others whom I trust and respect.
I invite you to listen carefully.

oo0oo

Jesus/Yeshua died.
Those close to him, we would claim, were both surprised and shattered.
Stricken with fear and grief, they were in no mood
to be looking for that 'silver lining'
that supposedly comes with every cloud.

As one of my early theology mentors put it:
"[they] saw he could never carry to fulfillment the mission of the Jewish people as they conceived it… They had thought he would save the world by making supreme over human existence the good as seen in the perspective of Jewish culture. Now they saw he never could do anything of the sort… They reached that depth of despair which come when all that seems to give hope to human existence is seen to be an illusion" *(Wieman 1946:43).*

There was fear. There was guilt. There was confusion.
The rulers had once again
"prevailed over the ruled. The urban elites of Jerusalem had gained an even tighter control of temple and Torah" *(Herzog 2000: 247).*

But later, the disciples thought more about his death. It mattered to them.
But only because his life mattered more...
So they began to speak of his death in ways that affirmed his life.

And they came to see his life stood for something so important
he was willing to give his life for it *(Patterson 2004).*

And that something was the vision of life called
the Empire or Realm of God.

Over time they too came to reaffirm their own commitment
to the values and vision stamped into his life
by his words and deeds.

They even believed that "in his words were God's words" *(Patterson 2004:127).*
And that his vision of a new Empire,
cultivated by him among them long before he died,
no executioner or cross could kill.

Jesus/Yeshua was dead. But he was not dead to them.
His spirit was still coursing through their veins *(Patterson 2004).*

Again, as my theology mentor has said, such 'spirit' or 'creativity'
can be explained as:
(i) the emerging of new perspectives;
(ii) the integrating of these new perspectives with previous ones;
(iii) the expanding of one's appreciable world, and
(iv) the widening and deepening of community *(Wieman 1946).*

Likewise, when we believe in this vision of a possible new empire,
we too can reaffirm our commitment to the values and vision,
and a 'resurrection' invitation,
to live life deeply and with zeal.

To be embraced by life, not scared of it. In all its particularity.
Because life must be concretely practised.
It must be 'a way of life'.

Perhaps it could be practised, shaped by these thoughts:
• How do we care for each other interpersonally in ways which do not suffocate and oppress?
• How is the well-being of our neighbour pursued in the complex problem of global hunger and international war?
• How are communities developed positively around respect and care for each person rather than around a common enemy?
• How are the systemic causes of non-love eliminated? *(Shea 1980)*

To live with these particularities coursing in our veins,
is to live in the spirit of the sage we call Jesus.

Because resurrection is not just a collection of religious stories about a so-called once-only event in the past.

"How many years was Easter Sunday?" asks Dom Crossan *(Crossan 1994).* Resurrection can and does happen every day when we are:

> "moved by sacred hope and convinced of the profound significance of each person as an infinitely precious being... [when] we dream and plan and implement positive change to enhance the well being of self, others, and the whole of creation... while also embracing and dealing with the reality of our imperfections and their impact on ourselves, others, and creation" *(Vosper 2004).*

ooOoo

So... on this Easter Day 2009, I invite you
to consider, either for the first time, or yet again:

- Easter reminds us we are called into deeper community.
- Life invites us to be startled by Easter, not scared by it.
- Resurrection is not an escape from death, but an invitation to live life with zeal.
- We are not alone in this life of faith.

Life is renewable.
The human spirit is indomitable.
A loving, caring existence is stronger than death itself.

**Notes:**

Crossan, J. D. *Jesus: A Revolutionary Biography.* New York: HarperCollins, 1994.
Herzog II, W. R. *Jesus, Justice, And The Reign of God. A Ministry of Liberation.* Louisville: Westminster John Knox Press, 2000.
Patterson, S. J. *Beyond The Passion. Rethinking The Death And Life Of Jesus.* Minneapolis: Fortress Press, 2004.
Scott, B. B. "Introduction" in B. B. Scott (ed) *The Resurrection Of Jesus. A Sourcebook.* Jesus Seminar Guides. Santa Rosa: Polebridge Press, 2008.
Shea, J. *Stories Of Faith.* Chicago: The Thomas More Press, 1988.
Vosper, G. "Easter Day Liturgy". Direct from the author, 2004. Used with permission.
Wieman, H. N. *The Source Of Human Good.* Carbondale: Southern Illinois University Press, 1946.

# Transformations on the Edge of Time

Easter 3, 2011
Luke 24:13-25

I find it all very strange.
How can you fail to recognise someone you know so well?
I frequently fail to remember names.
But I never—well, hardly ever—fail to recognise people I know well.

More than that, I often see people, perhaps on television,
who remind me of someone I know.
    A turn of the head.
    The facial features.
    A mannerism.
Something gives me a fleeting glimpse of someone I know.

Yet although their hearts burned within them while
the stranger was speaking, the two disciples in our Gospel story
    weren't even reminded of Jesus/Yeshua.

In view of the recent horrifying events of the trial and crucifixion,
I imagined Jesus would have been very much on their minds.
    Yet they noticed no resemblance at all
    between the stranger they met on the road, and Jesus.

So the risen (or post-Easter) Jesus was quite different
from the pre Easter Jesus!

The post-Easter Jesus was not a resuscitated corpse.
And the post-Easter Jesus was seen differently by different people,
    and recognised through different characteristics.

Mary Magdalen, our storyteller suggests,
only recognised him when he spoke her name.
The gathered disciples recognised him only when they looked at his wounds.
The Emmaus couple recognised him through the breaking of bread.

oo0oo

Let's stay within the bounds of Luke's story.
The journey to Emmaus must have been terrific for those disciples.
Simulating.
Fascinating.
Challenging.

Yet despite all the talk, all the stories, and so little of the meaning,
the two only recognised the stranger when he
stopped speaking and started doing.

And the thing he started doing, which enabled recognition
was breaking something and giving it to them.

According to many people, brokenness is a vital part
of Christian experience, because it strips away
all the layers,
all the veneer,
and reveals the real, trembling, naked, vulnerable person underneath.

That's why Jesus enjoyed the company of the social outcasts so much.
Because they were broken and vulnerable people who had no veneer left.
They used their energy
not to build defences around themselves,
not to create an acceptable social manner,
but simply to survive.

Fortunately, for most of us in Australia, this kind of 'brokenness'
is not a way of life. Most of us are not on the margins.
We may not be rich, but neither are we
dragged down by grinding poverty.

So for us, brokenness tends to come differently:
bereavement,
divorce,
redundancy,
serious illness,
unemployment,
are all occasions of our brokenness.

They are occasions of suffering, when energy is used simply for survival,
and there's no spare energy to worry about social niceties
or what other people may think.

oo0oo

What might Luke's story say to us?
We may each recognise Jesus/Yeshua in different ways, and
through different events.
So, it seems, did the disciples.

He may not appear in the form we expect.
He didn't for any of the disciples.

We may not be aware that we've been walking with him.
Neither were the two disciples on the road to Emmaus.
But all those who experienced the presentness of the post-Easter Jesus
were changed or transformed by the experience.

Now similar experiences can be had in many different situations.
Karl Peters is a retired Professor of Philosophy and Religion.
In his excellent (I reckon) little book *Spiritual Transformations*,
Peters tells of another such transforming experience.

I invite you to listen and reflect on his story:

> "Several years ago, I was driving down a street in Winter Park, Florida, on my way to a class… Winter Park has these lovely southern oak trees that create canopies over the streets. The sun was behind me, streaming down through the trees and giving everything a warm, early morning glow. As I drove, I was reflecting on a course I was teaching, a science and religion course on evolution and creation. I was thinking about the fourteen-billion-year history of the universe.
>
> "Suddenly I realized that I was on the edge, the edge of the universe. This was not the edge of space but the edge of time. I realized that the whole universe had taken fourteen billion years

to bring me, and everything else, to the moment I was in. All that time, all that creative activity bringing into being galaxies, stars, our planet Earth, life, and me. Wow! I was awestruck. I still am.

"We all are on the edge of time – right now, in every moment. Each of us is a special form of energy-matter that has been created through a series of transformations over fourteen billion years" *(Peters 2008:2-3)*.

oo0oo

As I was also checking out some sermon web sites I came across this comment.
Words which suggest some occasions
where we are likely to 'recognise' Jesus/Yeshua.

While traditional-sounding this particular suggestion
does offer a challenge.
Again, I invite your consideration:

'the risen Jesus is to be found in Galilee, among the flotsam and jetsam of society, where we least expect to find him.

'We are likely to find the risen Jesus at an AA meeting or among a group of people supporting an AIDS sufferer close to death. That is the sorts of places Jesus has already gone before us.

'We don't pray that he will be there... We don't take Jesus there by condescending to visit these unfortunates. We are bidden to gird up our loins and follow, to be enriched with the joy of finding the risen Jesus in new places doing new things.

'If we don't we will be simply left behind...'

And then this telling comment:

'And perhaps we might find him in the very last place we would expect - in our own lives - if you're anything like me, for I don't consider myself 'spiritual' or 'religious''.

We all are on the edge of time—right now, suggests Karl Peters.

"And on the edge of time, we are always going into the future. It is an unknown future. Yet it is a future upon which our thinking and actions will make a difference...What a responsibility! What kind of future are we being called to create?" *(Peters 2008:3).*

**Notes:**

Peters, K. E. *Spiritual Transformations. Science, Religion, And Human Becoming*. Minneapolis: Augsburg Fortress, 2008.

# Pentecost: A Day to See Green amid the Red!

Pentecost, 2009
Acts 2:1-8

A man whispered, "God speak to me!"
and a kookaburra laughed. But the man didn't hear.

So the man called out, "God speak to me!"
and thunder rolled across the sky. But the man didn't listen.

The man looked around and said, "God let me see you!"
and a star shone brightly. But the man didn't see.

Despairingly the man said, "God show me a miracle"
and a life was born. But the man didn't notice.

Desperate now, the man said, "Love me God",
and his wife smiled at him. But that was so normal, he missed it.

Feeling completely alone he whispered into the heavens,
"Touch me God and let me know you are here!"
    God reached down and touched the man.

But the man brushed the butterfly away and went sadly on his way *(Unknown)*.

oo0oo

Today is Pentecost Sunday.
    A day when most Christians see red!
    A day for being surprised and fully enlivened by Creativity God.

For Pentecost is about allowing the wind/spirit of Creativity God,
to fill every fibre of nature, and of our being,
    in every moment of our matter-energy, space-time, existence.

Like a "movie director" *(Loader 2006)*, Luke, the anonymous storyteller
we traditionally claim as the author of the *Acts of the Apostles*,
which we now reckon was written in the early 2nd century,
creates an imaginative scene of wind and fire... and noise.

A script full of symbolism which can not be taken literally,
whatever historical events may or may not lay behind the story.

On the other hand, Pentecost is also about
hearing and experiencing Creativity God
in a language we can understand.

Not just in Australian or French or German or any of the
Asian or Pacific or Aboriginal languages,
but also in the language of such social issues as
reconciliation,
un- and under-employment,
global marketing,
and the ecological crisis.

What a difference a day makes!

oo0oo

Some years ago, I read two very interesting articles,
published nearly 40 years apart, which I reckon can take the Pentecost story
beyond the 'language' game traditionalists are want to play,
into some of these real and important social concerns.

One article was on 'Religious Naturalism'
and our understanding of the natural world.
The other was on the ecological crisis as a 'spirit'-ual problem.

Unlikely subjects to be linked with Pentecost? Perhaps.
So let me weave some random thoughts
I gained from these articles.
And on Pentecost.

Lynn White Jr, in what is now his famous 1967 article called
"*The Historical Roots Of Our Ecological Crisis*", suggests that
Christianity's attack on so-called pagan religion
effectively stripped the natural world of any spiritual meaning.

Indeed, Christianity replaced the belief that the 'sacred' is in rivers and trees,
with the doctrine that God is a disembodied spirit
whose true residence is in heaven, not on earth.

He writes:

"By destroying pagan [religions], Christianity made it possible to exploit nature in a mood of indifference to the feelings of natural objects" *(White 1967).*

Mmm. What an interesting thought, I thought. So I read on.
The impact of Christianity's teachings has tended to empty the biosphere
of any sense of God's presence in natural things.

God, in terms of traditional theism, is pictured as a sky-God.
And in turn, human beings, as bearers of God's image,
are regarded essentially as 'souls' taking up
temporary residence in their earthly bodies.

So, White says, in this sense the ecological crisis:
global warming,
irreversible ozone depletion,
massive deforestation, is fundamentally a spiritual crisis.

Because... certain Christian teachings have blunted our ability
to experience co-belonging with other life forms.
And this has rendered us unwilling to alter our self-destructive course
and plot a new path toward sustainable living.

Simply put: we have forgotten the earth is alive,
filled with Creativity God—and worthy of our respect.

The second article, written by Roger Gillette,
a retired physicist and system development engineer,
suggests the term 'nature' should now cover:

"the whole complex, interrelated and interacting unitary universe of matter-energy in space-time, a universe of which humans are an integral part..." *(Gillette 2006:1).*

That is, the universe as a whole is, and must be, of intrinsic value, and each part:

galaxy,
organism,
individual atom,

participates in that intrinsic value as it participates in the universe.
Rather than separating one bit out as more important than the rest.

Again my interest was sparked.
But I admit to being slightly distracted at the time I read this article.
Five white, sulphur-crested cockatoos, were feeding
in a large Chinese Elm tree just outside my study window.

And they were having one giant Pentecost party,
squawking, and eating the seeds,
and snapping off the ends of the branches, resulting in
a ton of yellow tinged leaves and twigs
falling all over the lawn and paths below.

Tempting me as I mumbled a string of complaints,
to go get my trusty Canberra Autumn rake!

So when Gillette goes on to suggest that we can no longer think and feel that humans are separate from the 'environment'... He says:

"We must think and feel that we are part of and at one with the whole holy system we call the global ecosystem…" *(Gillette 2006:4).*

I reckoned he was challenging me to rethink
my thinking and feelings about my relationship with those cockatoos!

But Gillette's article pushes on.
For this thinking and feeling to genuinely happen, it will require all of us
to take the findings of modern science seriously, resulting in
"revolutionary change in world view (by) the world religious traditions... (for) it requires a radical spiritual transformation"
*(Gillette 2006:6).*

So, how is Pentecost moved beyond the traditional 'language' game?
As a progressive religious thinker, I would want to suggest...
Listening to both White and Gillette, Pentecost is
living with, rather than against, nature.

And listening to both White and Gillette, Pentecost implies
love, and love implies concern—for the well-being of the beloved...
For the whole of that 13.7 billion year old,
complex, matter-energy in space-time, called 'nature'.

Why, I reckon if we were to passionately live this,
others looking at us just might claim we were drunk!

Certainly we could claim to be "super, natural Christians" *(McFague 2000).*
Because, as Sallie McFague argues, it is commensurate
with the radical, destabilizing, inclusive love of Jesus.

oo0oo

Pentecost is more than a so-called past event.
It is the story of Creativity 'God'—who indwells and sustains all life forms.
Galaxy.
Organism.
Individual atom.

Not 'incarnate' in just one person, but becoming incarnate in all of us.
As we dream dreams and see a vision of
justice and compassion and ecological responsibility in the world.

Not in the babble of tongues, but in the gift of tongues.
The ability to hear and speak the hard word,
to understand it, to celebrate it, and to tell it in the
uniqueness of our own passionate living.

So how might Pentecost be understood today, in 21st century Canberra,
a few weeks after Earth Hour?

Perhaps by remembering:

> God the Spirit enfleshed in creation, [experiencing] the agony of an earth under siege. For the Spirit as the green face of God has become in our time the wounded God *(Unknown).*

And one of the ways we could take the initiative in all this, is to shape a more honest openness to nature... in all its fragility and variety.

For to live in harmony with nature
is to live inspired (in-spirited, in-the-Spirit) lives.

It's a different twist on Pentecost, I know.
Yet even the traditional story encourages and celebrates a certain freedom
to set out on new, open and uncharted roads.

So such a twist on Pentecost would be worth naming and celebrating, I reckon.
On any day. But especially on a religious day when
we need to see a touch of green amid all the red!

**Notes:**

Gillett, P. R. 2006. "Theology of, by, and for religious naturalism" in *Journal Of Liberal Religion* 6, 1, 1-6. (An online journal).

Loader, W. "First Thoughts on Gospel Passages from the Lectionary". http://wwwstaff.murdoch.edu.au/~loader/lectionaryindex.html Accessed May 2006.

McFague, S. *Super, Natural Christians*. Kindle Edition, 2000.

White, L. "The historical roots of our ecological crisis", http://www.zbi.ee/~kalevi/lwhite.htm Accessed 2006.

# Power Enabling rather than Power Over

Pentecost 5, 2012
Mark 6:1-13

Today we continue to be shaped by the stories
from the anonymous storyteller we call Mark.
The storyteller which most scholars now claim
was the earliest of all the Canon gospel storytellers.

And what an interesting storyteller this 'Mark' is!
Indeed, one who has spent a lifetime of academic study on Mark, says:
"When we enter the story world of the Gospel of Mark, we enter
a world full of conflict and suspense, a world of surprising reversals
and strange ironies, a world of riddles and hidden meanings...
[where] Jesus is the dominant character" *(Rhoads 1982:1, 101).*

Having now heard three or four of Mark's stories over the past few weeks
perhaps you have begun to sense some of that 'conflict'
and 'surprising reversals' and 'hidden meanings' too.

But having said that, let me have another look
at the stories which we have heard over the past two weeks:
the stilling of the storm,
the healing of the woman with the haemorrhage.

As well as today's stories:
a visit to the hometown, and the sending out of the disciples.

Many sub themes are interwoven into all these stories.
In all my comments these past couple of weeks
I have only touched on one or two of those themes.
There are several others.

Today's story highlights one such sub theme—'power'.
And of course this theme is also in the other stories as well.
Power over nature.
Power over illness.

But interestingly enough in today's stories,
'power' is experienced in deep contrast.
For Jesus/Yeshua, it was a limiting of power.
For the disciples, it was God's 'healing power' in others lives.
So let me stay with this 'power' sub theme for a bit
as I play back and forth between all these stories.

oo0oo

• In the story of the stilling of the storm...
Mark and other storytellers of the day
saw the ability to control the sea and subdue storms
as characteristic of having 'divine power' *(Nineham 1963:146).*

So when the storm hit the boat threatening to sink it,
the disciples don't just reproached Jesus for his seeming indifference.

As Waler Wink suggests, they attack him personally.
They project onto him concern for their well-being and survival,
and are thus emptied of the inner resources to deal with the
storm themselves.

Once awake, so the story goes, Jesus
"performed the characteristically divine act... and the disciples
were... filled with a different kind of fear... realizing they were in
the presence of one who disposed of power nothing less than
divine" *(Nineham 1963:147).*

• In the story of the woman with the haemorrhage...
For 12 years, so the storyteller says, a woman suffered from
a continuing loss of blood that clearly
debilitated body, resources, and morale.

In almost a last lunge for life, she thrusts her feeble fingers
toward the hem of Jesus' garment.
Then a 'power drain'.

She felt drained by the sheer energy of her action and confession.

He felt drained by the force of her need.

• In the story of the hometown visit...
As a result of the scepticism of his hometown family and neighbours,
our storyteller says Jesus' power to heal others was 'limited'.

What exactly is the tension between Jesus and his family, especially his brothers?
After all, writes New Testament scholar Dom Crossan,

> "[a]ny Mediterranean peasant would expect an expanding ripple of patronage-clientage to go out from Jesus, through his family and his village, to the outside world..." *(Crossan 1991:347).*

Well, these stories are certainly living out that earlier comment:

> "...a world of surprising reversals and strange ironies, a world of riddles and hidden meanings" *(Rhoads 1982:1).*

But one other story remains.
• The story of the sending out of the disciples...

And here I want to offer the comments of Process theologian, Bruce Epperly.
Mark the storyteller says Jesus/Yeshua sent his disciples out two by two.

> "Unlike the rulers of the earth", suggests Epperly, "they travel simply and affirm their need of others in order to live their vocation. Jesus' disciples are challenged to see their healing vocation as relational" *(Epperly 2006).*

And then this:

> "In the healing adventure, giving and receiving are interdependent. The generosity of others enables us to fulfill our vocations. The disciples accept hospitality, but also do not blame or punish those who turn their backs on them. They let go of failure, knowing that success is not entirely in their own hands. They can't control the belief or unbelief of others. Freed of the need to succeed, they simply go on to the next healing adventure. Great things happen!" *(Epperly 2006).*

Finally:

> "As God's partners in healing the world, we need to cultivate healthy models of relational power..." *(Epperly 2006).*

Mmm. I reckon it is in living out of a 'relational power' perspective
that we are helped to unlock the surprising reversals
    and strange ironies
    and the hidden meanings in Mark's stories.

So what is this 'relational power' process theologians talk about?
Relational power seems to be about having the ability
    to both absorb and exert an influence.

To influence others and to be influenced by others.
And where relationships play a constructive role
    in the creation of individuals and groups
    and in their subsequent freedom to be themselves.

Such power stands in sharp contrast to its opposite: 'unilateral power'.
And in **this** game, the institutional church is no exception.

In her book *With Or Without God*, Gretta Vosper *(Vosper 2008)*
makes a repeated point:
    the history of the church is about power.

That is, some people believing they had the power to control
what other people could think, or believe, or do,
were and are determined to call others 'into line'.
    And they have been doing so for more than 1600 years!

Now it is clear our storyteller Mark reckoned Jesus used 'power'.
    Sometimes that 'power' was a power <u>over</u>...
    Over demons, as shaped and understood by a pre-scientific cosmology.

But most times, and especially with people, that 'power' was power **enabling**...
    Enabling **others** to accomplish their hopes.
    Enabling **others** to widen their understanding.
    Enabling **others** to break through restrictive habits of thinking and seeing

"(and) in expanding the freedom of the hearer, and in persuasion with respect to how that freedom might be used" *(Cobb 1997:103).*

oo0oo

For every reason under the sun we can't go back into the story world of Mark.
But by continuing to experience our own 21st century story world,
and seeing and hearing and struggling with that world,
in all its political reality,
perhaps in our choices and in our behaviour, we can now
be better prepared to live more courageous and humane lives.

Of course there is the use of 'power' in our lives, especially if society is to function at all, but we need to be also aware

"that power is an invariably corrupting experience for humans" *(Holloway 2008: 137).*

So once again I am reminded of the wisdom of one who has, over the years, helped in shaping my theological thinking:

"The earth belongs, or ought to belong, to those who make the largest claims on life. The largest claims are not made nor are they makeable in the form of unilateral power. They are made by those who attempt to embody most fully the life of relational power, for they are claims made not only for themselves but on behalf of all peoples" *(Loomer 1976).*

And, I would add, because of our daily choices,
become 'good news' to both themselves and to others.

**Notes:**


Cobb Jr, J. B. *Reclaiming The Church. Where The Mainline Church Went Wrong And What To Do About It.* Louisville: John Knox Press, 1997.

Crossan, J. D. *The Historical Jesus. The Life Of A Mediterranean Jewish Peasant*. North Blackburn: CollinsDove, 1991.

Epperly, B. "Process & Faith Lectionary Commentary". Process & Faith web site. http://processandfaith.org/resources/lectionary-commentary/ Accessed 2006.

Holloway, R. *Between The Monster And The Saint. Reflections On The Human Condition*. Melbourne: Text Publishing, 2008.

Loomer, B. E.. "Two conceptions of power" in *Process Studies* 6, 1, 5-32. 1976.

Nineham, D. E. *Saint Mark*. Pelican New Testament Commentaries. Middlesex: Penguin, 1963.

Rhoads, D. & D. Michie. *Mark As Story. An Introduction To The Narrative Of The Gospel*. Minneapolis: Fortress Press, 1982.

Vosper, G. *With Or Without God. Why The Way We Live Is More Important Than What We Believe*. Toronto: HarperCollins, 2008.

# On Counting the Women and Children...

Pentecost 12, 2008
Matthew 14:13-21

Some stories stick in your memory!
Being a former journalist, one which I always recall concerns a conversation between a veteran broadcast journalist and a fledging reporter.

Edwin Diamond, a scholar of the media, tells it this way:

> I'm going to tell you a story and after I tell it, you will know all there is to know about television news...
>
> The executives of this station were watching all three news shows one night. There had been a fire in a Roman Catholic orphanage. One executive complained that a rival station had better film coverage. 'Their flames are higher than ours', he said. But another executive countered: 'Yes, but our nun is crying harder than theirs...'

Likewise, Matthew's so-called story of the 'Feeding of the 5,000' is, for me, another one of those stories which have stayed with me.
Primarily because it is incorrectly named.

You can bet your socks on it there were many more people present.
Indeed, in the NRSV translation of this story there is the phrase:
'And those who ate were about five thousand men,
besides women and children...' *(NRSV).*

Besides women and children...
Not counting women and children...
Thanks to Megan McKenna's suggestions
I have heard this phrase in such a way
it always makes an impression on me.

Being astute people I am sure you noticed that in many cases within our biblical tradition, the so-called 'unnamed people' are women?

Men... well they are carefully named: Matthew, John, Peter, James, Thomas.

But when it comes to women, the biblical storytellers
are not so careful in getting all their names.
In fact sometimes this carelessness is very obvious.

On the other hand, if we were to read a couple of stories
from the *Gospel of Mary*,
we would find the echoes of a rather modern approach:
Peter is speaking to the group about Mary…

> 'Has the Saviour spoken secretly to a woman and not openly so that we would all hear? Surely he did not wish to indicate that she is more worthy than we are?'

Not a 'carelessness' this time, but a total questioning of integrity!

Bringing it very much closer to home, feminist theologian Rosemary Radford Ruether, suggests the women get no credit because their work in providing this food is also not counted:

> "...the reason there was so much food was that all the women, as women are wont to do, brought picnic baskets, food enough for themselves, their children and one or two neighbours. So of course there was more than enough for all. But since the women and children were not counted, the gospel writer did not know where the food came from and presumed it was a miracle performed by Jesus" *(Ruether 1996).*

In our time people react to the phrase—'besides' or 'not counting'—
the women and children in different ways.
Some with laughter.
Others with anger, sadness, or disgust.

But if you are a woman—one of those whose efforts don't always count—
neat theological justifications or interpretations are of little help.

oo0oo

Megan McKenna, whom I have already mentioned,
is a Catholic laywoman who has written on this story.
Let me share some of her suggestions...

She says such a phrase "besides" or "not counting" women and children can mean literally that... But it can also mean the sick,
the elderly,
the prostitutes,
the separated and divorced,
lepers,
tax collectors,
the strangers,
Gentiles and outcasts within Jewish society.

"It means," she writes, "the bulk of the crowd, the majority of the throng of people who are the followers of Jesus, desperately in need of good news, of caring, and of being fed and given attention, love, dignity, understanding, and hope for the future"
*(McKenna 1994:16).*

Notice how they are all people who have little hope!

Well, how can we, members of a religious community,
the majority of whom are women,
connect with a story which does not 'count' the women and children?

Learning much from Megan McKenna, I offer two comments.
You may wish to consider them.

• As a church community may I suggest we need to look at priorities:
in budgets,
in ethical decisions,
in politics and programs.

We must start not with the 5,000 who make sure they are counted, heard from, and included... those already 'in the club'.
Rather we must look to the vast majority
not counted,
not numbered,
not remembered.

And that may mean speaking out against government policies
in all the contentious areas decision making.

• And as a local congregation may I suggest
we need to look for those who are not included:

the unemployed,
those with mental illness,
the overseas adult student,
the religious 'exile'...

oo0oo

That is what the 'good news' is about.
What this story is about.
What Matthew's Jesus is about.
What ministry is about.

But perhaps the last word deserves to be given to Megan McKenna.
McKenna says:

> "...there are all kinds of levels in understanding (this story). But it is an adage that the one that is most true is the one that calls a person to a more radical following of Jesus" *(McKenna 1994:28).*

**Notes:**

McKenna, M. *Not Counting The Women And Children. Neglected Stories From The Bible*. Tunbridge Wells: Burns & Oates, 1994.
Ruether, R. R. "Matthew 14: 13-21". 1996. www.looksmart.com Accessed 2008.
*Holy Bible. NRSV*. Nashville: Thomas Nelson Publishers, 1989.

# Fear and 'Stony Ground' in Times of Change...

Pentecost 13, 2011
Matthew 14:22-33

With Matthew's fictional Jesus story still ringing in our ears,
I want to share with you a couple of contemporary cameos.

The first one is influenced by the world renowned psychologist,
Abraham Maslow.

> "One day [Maslow] asked his students: 'Which of you expects to achieve greatness in your chosen field?' The class looked at him blankly. After a long silence, Maslow said: 'If not you—*who* then?' [Only then] they began to see his point" *(Wilson 1972: 15).*

The second again comes from the world of psychology, from Eric Fromm.

> "...the real crisis of today is one that is unique in human history: it is the *crisis of life itself*... We are confronted with the probability that within fifty years – and perhaps much sooner—life on this earth will have ceased to exist; not only because of nuclear, chemical and biological warfare... but also because technological 'progress' makes the soil, the water and the air unfit for the sustenance of life... However who can give up hope as long as there is life? Who can be silent as long as there are billions of human beings, living, breathing, laughing, crying and hoping" *(Fromm 1970:159).*

I hope these cameos might serve as the matrix
for some comments I want to offer today
about the anonymous storyteller we call Matthew
and the particular 'Peter' story we heard from Matthew this morning.

oo0oo

Generally speaking, the anonymous writer of Matthew's gospel had a problem.
How to reshape and enlarge the number of Jesus stories
so the Jewish Jesus Movement members of his Syrian church
could hear them anew,
could be reassured against the likes of Paul,
and could grow in their faith.

When the writer of Matthew's gospel was shaping his material,
his small community was facing significant change.
Their society was changing... becoming multicultural.
So they had to stay the course, and both preserve
and develop their own authentic niche identity.

Could they achieve their goals? Even continue as a movement?
From where could they find the energy to hope?
Or would they succumb to their fears?
And if so, fears or fear of what?

Change was indeed happening all around them.
The Temple was gone. Judaism was being reshaped.
A bloke called Paul was gaining both Jewish and 'god-fearers' converts
to his personal "mystical experience" *(Wilson 2008:126)* movement.

The Jewish Jesus Movement was having battles on all fronts.

And so with a copy of what we call the Gospel of Mark in front of him,
along with some other writings we now call The 'Q' Gospel, and maybe
even bits of Paul's letter to the Galatians espousing his 'new religion',
Matthew sets out to tell his version of the Jesus Movement story,
some 50 years after the 'new Moses', called Jesus/Yeshua,
and some 20+ years after Paul.

And to give his story extra meaning, he often talks about some of the
so-called heroes of the Jesus Movement,
especially Simon, or Peter.
But never about Paul of the Christ Movement.

oo0oo

Simon is an interesting, if not complicated, sort of bloke.
He seems to believe and disbelieve in almost the same moment.
'Trust' and 'fear' coexist within him, as does
'faith' and 'little faith'.

So it is interesting if not a little ironic that he was given the nickname 'Petros' or 'rock', or perhaps more accurately, 'stony ground'.

Tradition says his origins were ordinary.
He left his home, his wife, his livelihood, to follow.

Australian sociologist John Carroll says of Simon:

> "When Simon the fisherman was called to follow, he heard the word with joy. But the forewarning is that he has no roots, so the moment there is stress, or fear... he will wither" *(Carroll 2007:31).*

Unfortunately all this gets lost in the English King James version of his name—Peter.
And lost, because Simon has been put on a theological pedestal,
at least by Matthew and those who followed him.

For it is Matthew, as we will hear in a couple of weeks time,
who says Peter the 'rock' will be the 'foundation stone'
on which the church is to be built!

Sure Simon was there for all the teaching and all the so-called 'miracles'.
But the real question is: what *did* he hear? Will he *learn*? Will he *understand*?
What if the 'rock' is indeed 'stony ground'
as the earlier parable of The Sower suggests?

Again John Carroll is suggestive:

> "[Simon] had responded with enthusiasm and joy to the call to become a fisher of men; but, as he has no roots... he withers. He exemplifies what it is to have no roots. Weak characters wilt under pressure. Boldness is not enough, if there is no anchor... On stony ground, men stumble" *(Carroll 2007:138, 139).*

Or as the biblical scholar Walter Wink has said:
we fall in love with our mentors or set them on pedestals,
refusing to see their flaws and regard them as bigger than life.

o0oo

In this morning's story, water has become Peter's 'stony ground'
rather than proof of Jesus' divine identity.
Simon is afraid.

Initially bold, under pressure he has lost his courage.
He had developed a dependency on Jesus.

Matthew's Jesus seems to respond by saying to Simon:
Confront your fears.
Forget your dependency.
You have the resources.
Don't be terrified of life.
Exercise your own faith!

Could this be the answer to one of my series of questions earlier on:
Fear of what?

oo0oo

Abraham Maslow asked his students:
which of you expects to achieve greatness in your chosen field?

Eric Fromm says the real crisis of today is one that is unique in human history:
it is the crisis of life itself.

Matthew's story, I reckon, was told to encourage the community of his day to:
Confront your fears.
Don't be terrified of life.
You have the resources.
Maintain your links to the 'historical' Jewish Jesus/Yeshua.

Matthew's story can also encourage our church community today,
in its time of pending change... if we
are open and honest and courageous enough to let it.

**Notes:**

Carroll, J. *The Existential Jesus*. Melbourne: Scribe Publications, 2007.
Fromm, E. *The Crisis Of Pychoanalysis. Essays On Freud, Marx, And Social Psychology*. New York: Holt, Rinehart, Winston, 1970.
Schweizer, E. *The Good News According To Matthew*. London: SPCK, 1975.
Wilson, B. *How Jesus Became Christian*. Toronto: Random House, 2008.
Wilson, C. *New Pathways In Psychology. Maslow And The Post-Freudian Revolution*. London: Victor Gollancz, 1972.

# A Ban on Divorce or a Ban on Legalism?

Pentecost 17, 2012
Mark 10:2-16

I have only ever preached on the first part of today's story from Mark,
—the bit about divorce—a couple of times.

I no longer have a copy of the original sermon.
But a faded newspaper report of my sermon
indicates the first time was during my first placement
in Ballarat (Australia), nearly 40 years ago.

It was around that time the then Federal government
was introducing significant changes to the divorce laws.

Those who were opposed to divorce, including the then
Catholic Archbishop of Melbourne, Dr James Knox,
were pounding the beat to every newspaper and radio station,
complaining, arguing, legalising.

So I ventured in with my two bobs worth.
Now, here I go again!

oo0oo

Today's story has words that are likely to make us cringe.
Generally speaking it can be hard to hear them as good news!
For to talk about divorce can open for many people,
a whole range of different wounds and experiences.
Shock.
Hurt.
Confusion.
Anger.
Frustration.
And I think I know most of you well enough to be able to say that

for some of you those feelings have been yours, personally,
or the feelings of family members whom you love.
So me responding to the first part of our gospel story,
rather than skipping over it to the assumed safe, second part,
may bring back some of those feelings again.

While I would regret that, I hope what I do say will be both honest and gentle.

oo0oo

To begin with let's look at this biblical story.
It seems to be set within a legal debate with some of the Pharisees.
That's important to note.
And a legal debate about men's rights, not everyone's rights.

While it is always difficult to recover the authentic words of Jesus
it would appear that many scholars feel Mark's comments,
along with some other biblical references as well,
makes it highly likely that Jesus did have something to say on
divorce,
marriage,
the family.
That's the first thing I want to say.

The second thing is early Christians found those comments difficult.
Because it seems some people did leave—divorce—their families
to join the Jesus movement,
with all the consequences such an action brought with it in that society.

And, they also heard those words as Jesus establishing
a new and even more impossible law
to replace the already impossible Mosaic law.

That is, Jesus' reply was heard as a legal reply to a legal question.
But what if the reply is not about 'legals'?

With the help of a colleague's suggestion, let's play it back.
"Is it lawful... they ask.
"What did Moses' law say?" he asks.
"Well, here's chapter and verse..." they reply.

And Jesus, as always, would say:
"Look beyond your petty nasty human laws which are about failure and exclusion and not about joy and gladness for all.

"Look into our 'original blessings' before our 'original failures', to the way God intended human beings
to relate to each other,
to seek their true selves, and
to find their true joys..."

That has a different ring to it!
And it can certainly put the debate into a different arena!
Beyond men's rights.
And in Jesus' time that was totally unheard of!

Bruce Prewer in his comments on this story, says:

"I believe that at one level, Jesus was confronting the male arrogance which had made divorce primarily a male privilege. He was angry with their treatment of women. His words about divorce and the hardness of men's hearts are a social justice protest.

"But even more they are a protest against moral and religious legalism, which does not put you closer to God but further away. Jesus was not putting a ban on divorce. He was putting a ban on self righteousness" *(B Prewer)*

Most people find the naming of separation or divorce, difficult.
Those who have gone through a divorce know it is much more than
just falling out of love beyond the point of no return.

When I asked a person who had been divorced
to read my sermon and comment on it, her response was:
"Few of us really know what goes on in each others' marriages. But people do not divorce without good reason. Divorce demands courage from all involved. It hurts. But it can also release".

For some divorce can be an act of destruction. For others it is a sense of release.
All certainly don't need a legalistic church
or a bunch of literalist clergy,
to add to the hurt or difficulties.

When a marriage fails, people need help and support
to leave the relationship without
        rancour,
        bitterness,
        hostility,
        fear.
Certainly with mutual dignity and respect.

But perhaps that's already too much on this story...

oo0oo

There is the second story in our Lectionary reading.
Mothers bringing children to Jesus.
        But why were they bringing children to him?
        Why do they want Jesus to touch them?
        Why were the disciples wanting to 'shoo' them away?

I am helped by two suggestions.
The first suggestion is of a mental picture of this story.
        A picture not at all like so many paintings of Jesus and children,
        where all the children have a squeaky-clean look.

Children full of life and smiles,
like the one that hung, framed, beside the framed Cradle Roll
        in my childhood Sunday School.

Rather, the mental picture is more like
the emergency room at a children's hospital.

Jesus is surrounded by sick children
and all the problems and smells that come with that:
        runny noses and dirty faces,
        diarrhoea and smelly nappies,
        crying or whimpering that just won't stop.

With this picture in mind,
it makes more sense to think that the disciples
        would want to protect Jesus from these sick children.
Somebody like Jesus wouldn't want to waste time with sick children!

He'd have more important things to do!
Wouldn't he?

The second suggestion is less graphic.
The disciples shooing away the children is also
a case of 'separation' or 'divorce'.
Divorce between the children and Jesus.

According to one overseas colleague, he suggests that
this whole section in Mark's story can be seen as a discourse
on the intention of God to bring together, not to separate.

Then he asks these challenging questions:
Where is the church still acting like the disciples
in separating people from Jesus?
Is it with those oriented toward their own gender?
Is it with the poor and homeless, the lonely and lost?
Is it with immigrants or the mentally ill?

oo0oo

Much of Jesus' energy in controversy with his fellow country-people
was spent trying to show that we must interpret scripture in a way
which sees its priority as concern for human well being.

So despite all the ink and paper and hot air
given to arguments against divorce,
I reckon the simple 'good news' of these stories is,
any so called ban needs to be on legalism
rather than on broken relationships.

**Notes:**

Bruce Prewer."Resources for Worship". Now found at: http://www.bruceprewer.com/b_rcl.htm Accessed in June/July 2000 and 2003.

# Doers Rather than Caught in the Spell of Good Intentions Only

Pentecost 20, 2008
Matthew 21:28-32

George Burns, the late American comedian, was at one time recorded as offering preachers some so-called 'good' advice. He said:
'A good sermon should have a good beginning and a good ending, and they should be as close together as possible' *(Bausch 1996:12).*

Yes, I am sure we all have our own 'preachers' jokes!
And yes, preaching 'week in, week out',
can sometimes be a bit of a challenge!

Well, today's story from the bloke we call Matthew is,
I reckon, going to be one such occasion.
A bit of a challenge.

Because there seems to be a fair amount of confusion
around who actually says 'yes' in the story,
and what meaning, if any, we might give to it all.

ooOoo

Let's revisit the story which we have just heard.
Stories of two sons are a staple diet of Jewish tradition.
I am sure you can recall at least a couple.

In Matthew's Jesus story, a man orders one of his sons to work in the vineyard.
He says 'I will not,' but has a change of heart and goes to work.

The other son immediately says yes, but never goes to the vineyard.

The parable leaves us wondering what the father would do
and what happens to the deceptive son.

But… and yes there is a but.
But Matthew's Jesus interrupts with a question:
Which of the two **did** the father's will?

Now I am reliably informed by several biblical scholars there are at least three different versions of this story.
And so you might engage with all this a little differently,
I have printed those three versions on the Liturgy sheets.

<u>Version 1</u>

| | |
|---|---|
| 1st son: | Says 'yes'. Doesn't move |
| 2nd son: | Says 'no'. Latter goes |
| Right answer: | Second |

<u>Version 2</u>

| | |
|---|---|
| 1st son: | Says 'no'. Later goes |
| 2nd son: | Says 'yes'. Doesn't move |
| Right answer: | First |

<u>Version 3</u>

| | |
|---|---|
| 1st son: | Says 'no'. Later goes |
| 2nd son: | Says 'yes'. Doesn't move |
| Right answer: | Second |

Perhaps you might like to have a quick chat with the person next to you about these three versions.

*(Conversation)*

OK. Because there are so many versions of this story
we can't be absolutely sure of its original form.
However many scholars, from what I can discover,
suggest Version 1 is probably "the correct text" *(Funk & Hoover 1993:232).*

But… Matthew's story ending doesn't always follow the story plot.
And… it also depends on the matrix or context of the story
and the accompanying interpretation.

Despite all this, I thought I might offer some brief comments of two scho...
to go with your own comments during that time
of discussion we had earlier.

The first scholar comes from the 19th century
and he is called Soren Kierkegaard.
The second comes from the 20th century
and she is called Barbara Reid.

Kierkegaard was born in Copenhagen, Denmark,
and is recognised as an outstanding philosopher, theologian,
literary critic, poet and psychologist.

Among those 20th century theologians
who have been influenced by his thinking, are:
Dietrich Bonhoeffer, Rudolf Bultmann,
Martin Buber and Paul Tillich.

And Kierkegaard's matrix or context was a life-time argument,
even bitter argument, he had with the Danish State Church of his time.

In 'Under the spell of good intentions' Kierkegaard asks:
what is the 'point' *(as if there is only one point)* of this parable?

So he writes:

> "Is it not meant to show us the danger of saying 'Yes' in too great a hurry, even if it is well meant?... It is easy to think that by making a promise you have at least done part of what you promised to do, as if the promise itself were something of value. Not at all! In fact, when you do not do what you promise, it is a long way back to the truth. Beware! The 'Yes' of promise keeping is sleep-inducing. An honest 'No' possesses much more promise... Ah, it is all too true that 'the road to hell is paved with good intentions'"
> *(Bruderhof Communities).*

I invite you to ponder Kierkegaard's comments for a moment.

*(Silence)*

Barbara Reid is a Dominican sister and distinguished professor of
New Testament at the Catholic Theological Union in Chicago.
Her several books and work on the parables
makes current feminist biblical scholarship
available to preachers, teachers, and pastoral ministers.

Her comments are, I reckon, insightful:

> "At first the parable seems a simple, straightforward one. Both children fall short of the ideal, but when Jesus asks which of the two **did** the father's will, the answer seems easy: the first. In a culture that highly prizes honor, however, it is not so very clear which child is the more laudable. The first one shamed his father by refusing to go. The second says the honorable thing, even if his actions do not conform" *(Reid 2001:156).*

While later on she says:

> "Neither child had it all together. But the one who had the humility to change their mind and do what was asked was the exemplary one. [So] are there ways in which, both as individuals and as a community, we are being asked to admit we were wrong and then embark on a new course of action?" *(Reid 2001:161).*

Again I invite you to ponder these comments just a little.

*(Silence)*

oo0oo

When the writer of Matthew's gospel was shaping this material,
his small community in Syria was facing significant issues.
Their society was changing... becoming more multicultural.
So they had to stay the course, and both
preserve and develop their own authentic niche identity.

Generally speaking, the Jesus Movement was having battles on all fronts.
The Temple in Jerusalem was gone.
Judaism was being reshaped.

And a bloke called Paul was gaining both Jewish and 'god-fearer' converts to his personal "mystical experience" movement *(Wilson 2008:126).*

Perhaps the 'good beginning' and the 'good ending' of his sermons and public comments, were stretching out even further apart!

But more than likely, as it was with the community's hero, Simon, nicknamed 'stony ground'... maybe
the small community was composed of people who,
in times of persecution and stress, had said 'No'.
And were now being invited to rejoin by saying 'Yes'.

As another commentator on this story suggests:

> "Matthew's community is not the heir of powerful religious leaders who prided themselves on their honorific titles and stunning interpretations of Torah, but of tax collectors (members of [an occupation] forbidden to observant Jews) and women so oppressed that they sell their very selves. It is people like these who say yes and become 'doers' of God's will" *(Donahue 2008).*

Perhaps we still have a lot more pondering to do on this extraordinary story.

**Notes:**

Bausch, W. J. *Storytelling The Word. Homilies And How To Write Them.* Mystic: Twenty-Third Publications, 1996.

Donahue, J. An article in *America. The National Catholic Weekly* web site. http://www.americamagazine.org/ Accessed October 2008.

Funk, R. & R. Hoover. *The Five Gospels. The Search For The Authentic Words Of Jesus.* New York: Macmillan, 1993.

Kierkegaard, S. "Under the spell of good intentions". Bruderhof Communities web site. http://www.bruderhof.com/ Accessed October 2008

Reid, B. E. *Parables For Preachers. The Gospel Of Matthew.* Year A. Collegeville:The Liturgical Press, 2001.

Wilson, B. *How Jesus Became Christian.* Toronto: Random House, 2008.

# Taxes Might Go to Caesar, but Thanks for the Pocket-money!

Pentecost 23, 2008
Matthew 22:15-21

Matthew's story of the conversation around the image on a coin
is one of the most famous of all anecdotes told about Jesus.
And I just luv it!

And one that, many scholars claim, is frequently misunderstood,
or imagined in unnecessary ways.

It has also been used by some, including politicians, to justify
a separation of the affairs of religion
and the affairs of commerce and government.

That the church ought not to be involved in anything
that has to do with politics... Religion is for the private sphere.
Well, that is always claimed before an election!

So let's explore this really radical story a bit.
And to begin with, I need to once again
place this story in its cultural contexts.

oo0oo

The immediate context provided by the anonymous storyteller
we call Matthew seems to be the ongoing 'wrestle' between
the leading Jewish scholars of the day,
and the itinerant sage, Jesus of Nazareth.

And this 'wrestling' is done in a very traditional way:
ask a question; get a response, usually a story; ask another question.

Matthew also makes it fairly clear that from his perspective,
this questioning was being done in the hope
Jesus' answers would undermine his standing
with the general population.

The background context is similar to many of the other stories told by Jesus.
(i) rural land was being taken over by big city, rich landlords,
meant small farm owners were losing their land;
(ii) mounting debt, payable to both Roman officials and priestly aristocracy,
meant the crisis of debt and dispossession grew deeper;
(iii) farmer labourers were being forced onto the unemployment line, and
(iv) a new Roman taxation system was extracting nearly every last cent.
The atmosphere was potentially explosive.

Theologian John Cobb's comment is helpful at this point:

> "Taxes are never popular, but when a subjugated people are forced to pay taxes to a foreign overlord, the taxes are especially hateful" *(Cobb 2008).*

So to raise a question about the controversial matter of taxes,
would create immediate interest and conversation then, as it does now.

But this question is a two-edged sword.
Again John Cobb's comment is, I reckon, helpful:

> "[A response] that they should cease to pay taxes would be revolutionary. Since their resistance would be met by military force, those who refused would either be martyred or they would fight. For Jesus to encourage non-payment of taxes would be incitement to violence.
>
> "On the other hand, if a religious teacher such as Jesus encouraged accepting Roman rule, that could well alienate the resentful. Truly to believe in God and God's choice of the people of Israel suggested that God would liberate the Jews if they rose up righteously. Counselling acceptance seemed a kind of betrayal" *(Cobb 2008).*

oo0oo

"Tell us what you reckon: Is it lawful to pay taxes
to the Roman emperor, or not?"

So Matthew goes on to tell how Jesus
turned the challenge back on his questioners,
thus avoiding entrapment, with two moves.

First, he asked for a coin.
When his questioners produced one, Jesus looked at it and asked,
Whose image is this? Whose name is on it?

Second, his response, with a dismissive shrug of the shoulders:
Pay the emperor what belongs to the emperor,
and God what belongs to God!

Not a pronouncement about the legitimacy of Roman imperial rule
or taxation or political authority.

> "...paying money to Caesar was a trivial affair in comparison with giving to God what belonged to God,", suggests John Cobb *(Cobb 2008).*
>
> "His response was never meant to be figured out. Rather... we see his deft debating skill," suggests Marcus Borg *(Borg 2003).*

An imaginative and brilliant way of evading entrapment.
Mmm.

oo0oo

Now, I want to suggest again that if we are to hear this story
in the way Borg and others suggest,
we will have to use our imaginations differently
and hear the story afresh.

Three people who are able to help us stretch our imaginations
in different directions, are:
Doug Adams, Robert Funk and Rabbi Arthur Waskow.

I have introduced their suggestions before. So you will have heard them.
But I reckon they are so good I want to share them again.
All hear much 'humour' in this story. Yes, humour!

oo0oo

Doug Adams noted that when Jesus asks the Pharisees
to produce a coin, they do so... *(Ask for a coin)*
Even though a strictly pious Jew
would never carry a coin bearing the emperor's image
with an inscription proclaiming him to be king and God!

These presumed righteous citizens are thus carrying around coins
that break two commandments!
The behaviour of the Pharisees, is incriminating,
embarrassing,
and amusing, to say the least.
And certainly noted by all the ordinary people
who have had to 'toe the line'!

Robert Funk suggested there was no indication that Jesus
returned the coin to the Pharisees.

According to Funk, as Jesus proclaims the punch line
'and (pay) God what belongs to God!'
he pockets the coin and has the last laugh *(Funk & Hoover 1993:526).*
*(I too would pocket the coin/note)*

Meanwhile, Rabbi Arthur Waskow imaginatively adds
another line to the story:
'Whose image is on the coin?
'The emperor's?
Jesus puts his arm on the troublemaker's shoulder and asks:
'And whose image is on this coin?' *(Waskow 2008).*

Listen as Rabbi Arthur Waskow continues:

> "Jesus has not proposed dividing up the turf between the material and the spiritual. He has redefined the issue: 'Give your whole self to the One who has imprinted divinity upon you! You, a fellow rabbi, know that is the point of this story. All I have done is remind you'" *(Waskow 2008).*

Humour and debating skills and some deeper meaning
by a skilful peasant sage.
Not guidance for taxation or political authority.

But... and yes, there is still a 'but'.
It does raise the provocative and still relevant question:
what if 'the emperor' is vile and violent Mugabe,
or school yard bullies,
or global capitalism,
or al Qeada?

Perhaps we still need to ponder this story some more!

**Notes:**

Borg, M. Seeing the Bible Again. 'What belongs to God?' Beliefnet web site. http://www.beliefnet.com/ Accessed 2003.

Cobb Jr, J. B. "Process & Faith Lectionary Commentary". Process & Faith web site. http://processandfaith.org/resources/lectionary-commentary/. Accessed 2008.

Funk, R. W. & R. W. Hoover. *The Five Gospels. The Search For The Authentic Words Of Jesus*. New York: MacMillan Press, 1993.

Waskow, A. 'What is "the image of God?"'. The Shalom Center Web site. https://theshalomcenter.org/ Accessed 2008.

# The 'Talent' of Being a Whistleblower

Pentecost 27, 2008
Matthew 25:14-30

The story of "The talents' is a very powerful story.
It is one of those stories that has left its mark
on our language and culture in a big way.

So much has it become part of our everyday vocabulary,
we tend to miss the 'fang' or 'twist' hidden in its tail.
And that's a pity.

oo0oo

How can we connect with this story, this parable?

Some scholars suggest we can connect through the story's ecclesiastical context.
And Matthew's context is one of the great church debates of his, and our, day.
• Should we stay as we are? Or should we change…
• Become more of an inclusive community
and let 'the others', the Gentiles, people who are different, in?

Supporting this view, West Australian theologian Bill Loader, says
Matthew's church is probably remembering:

> "the controversy over the expansion of the gospel into the Gentile world and the refusal of some… to accept that the doors should be flung open so recklessly... God is misbehaving again and they cannot believe it and refuse to support the adventure" *(Loader 2005).*

On the other hand much of our traditional interpretations or thinking
about the parable sees two servants being made heroes.

And they are rewarded by the owner because they have
faithfully engaged in various activities, such as
collecting tolls, interest, and other charges,
that have made the owner a profit.

Such interpretations have, I reckon, turned this parable into an example story. Go and do likewise. Grow your gifts.

Or even more problematic: If you do well, God will grow your gifts!
Both blunt the sharp edge of this parable.

But there is yet another way of hearing this parable, which I reckon, is closer to the parable itself...

A story which really upsets our accepted world views.

And it is the view offered by scholars Wm Herzog 11 and Barbara Reid.

That is, the third servant, and not the other two, is the hero.
So let me offer some comments accordingly.

oo0oo

The parable gives the third servant as much space or attention as the other two servants put together.

And he is the real hero, because he challenges the system rather than accepting the system *(Herzog 1994:164).*

He does not go along with the money-raising, greed, and exploitation of both the owner and the other two servants.

And he tells the owner as much!

Now part of our problem is, when we hear this parable,

we tend hear it through 'capitalist' ears, which views wealth as something that can be increased by hard work or investment.

But in the social world of the parable, both in its original oral telling and in its later written form by storyteller Matthew,

it is thought there is only so much wealth.

An increase to one person takes away from another.

Let me share some of what Barbara Reid says on this:

> "From this perspective, the man who expects his money to be increased is the wicked one, who is unfettered in his greed...
> "The third servant, then, is not wicked (or incompetent), except in the eyes of those who are greedy acquisitors or those who are co-opted by them, as are the first two servants. The third [servant]

is the one who acted honorably by blowing the whistle on the wickedness of the [owner]...

"The parable is a warning to the rich to stop exploiting the poor and is one that encourages poor people to take measures that expose such greed for the sin that it is" *(Reid 2001:207-208).*

The owner is a tough, ruthless, seemingly all powerful businessman.
He doesn't care how he gets his profit
so long as he gets it—more often than not
from the poor, the unemployed, the landless.

The other two servants follow in this accepted pattern.

But the third names this as exploitation and will not participate in it.
He is a whistleblower on greed and corruption
against the abuse of power over the powerless - the poor.

But like most, if not all, whistleblowers,
having spoken the truth he is totally vulnerable.
Vilified.
Shamed.
Humiliated.

What a way to turn expectations and interpretations upside down!
From reward to exposing.
From self interest to another's interest.

But I reckon this was Jesus' teaching style.
To create an audience debate if you like:
between Roman pro-interest tradition
verses Jewish anti-interest tradition.

Mmm.
Whose 'law' does an audience member follow?

Interestingly enough, Matthew's Jesus seems to be saying
it is when we have the courage to name exploitation for what it is,
rather than to seek the reward,
we are re-imagining the world,
as is the realm of God imagined.

Hearing the story this way can make
the powerful angry and defensive, and
the powerless empowered!

oo0oo

Parables are stories which turn our world views upside down.
But what is the world view the parable wants to turn upside down?
I invite you to ponder that important question some time.

Because which world we view can make all the difference
to how we live in the present
and claim the future.

Will the connection be through the world-church institution?
If so, is the future to be claimed by
preserving, holding on to, staying the same?

Or is it claimed in freedom of action, acting boldly, changing?

Will the connection be through the world-global and social?
If so, is the future to be claimed through
a new interconnectedness of all life,
and the sustainability of resources?

Or is it global commercialism, international corporations
and third-world debt?

I invite you to ponder some more.

**Notes:**

Herzog II, W. R. *Parables As Subversive Speech. Jesus As Pedagogue Of The Oppressed*. Louisville: Westminster John Knox Press, 1994.

Loader, W. "First Thoughts on Gospel Passages from the Lectionary". http://wwwstaff.murdoch.edu.au/~loader/lectionaryindex.html. Accessed November 2005.

Reid, B. E. *Parables For Preachers. The Gospel Of Matthew*. Year A. Collegeville: The Liturgical Press, 2001.

# At the Gates, Bearing the Passion of the Christ...

Reign of Christ, 2006
John 18:33-38

Wow! What a great story!
A rich tapestry of a scene fraught with drama and colour
as the two protagonists square off.

Picture the storytellers scene.
Pilate is nervous. In his heart he knows Jesus is innocent.
In his mind he knows he must play the game of politics.
So he mixes up a compromise, washes his hands
of the whole affair, and sends Jesus off to his death...

Well, that's the way I commenced my sermon six years ago on this day,
the Reign of Christ, or as it is traditionally know, Christ the King.
A relatively recent liturgical commemoration, as liturgy goes,
instituted by Pope Pius XI in 1925 to celebrate the jubilee year,
and the 16th centenary of the Council of Nicea.

It was also a political statement as it affirmed the primacy of Christ
in the face of rising nationalism and fascism.

But since my sermon there's been Mel Gibson's film, *The Passion of The Christ*, and just recently, Andrew Denton's *God On My Side*.
And I've had a rethink.

So let me take a few steps back.

oo0oo

In early 2003, before Mel Gibson's film *The Passion of The Christ* was released, a group of seven scholars—four Catholic Christians and three Jews—
received and reviewed the script.

They sent a confidential report to Gibson one month later outlining their concerns and suggesting six major points,
they considered, should be reconsidered.

The first four points addressed concerns

> "arising from the steady round of publicity long before the film opened... that *The Passion of the Christ* was the most authentic representation of the Passion ever produced" *(Boys 2003).*

The scholars concluded:

(i) a film based on the script we read would promote anti-Semitism because of its virtually inexorable portrayal of Jews as blood-thirsty enemies of Jesus;
(ii) the script contained significant historical errors;
(iii) Jesus' opponents were one-dimensional 'bad guys,' with the drama and pathos driven almost entirely by violence; and
(iv) the portrayal of the person and mission of Jesus was partial and skewed.

The two additional points addressed various media reports depicting Mel Gibson as a 'good Catholic':

(v) the script drew upon New Testament texts without regard for... principles of biblical interpretation; and
(vi) *The Passion of The Christ* violated many significant Catholic teaching documents about interpreting the Passion and death of Jesus.

Some months later their comments were made public. The scholars reported:

> "In retrospect, we were incredibly naïve. We did not anticipate how readily *Icon Productions* (Gibson's company) would manipulate our report while refusing to address its substantive claims. Nor in our wildest dreams could we have envisioned the intensity of media interest our confidential (albeit unsolicited) advice to Mel Gibson would generate—thereby inviting condemnation from many of Gibson's fans" *(Boys 2003).*

The following edited eMail was representative of those received:

> "... *The Passion* is no more than a visual representation of GOSPEL

> truth, how dare [you] label this modern-day work of religious art (on the level of the Sistine Chapel) as a hate crime... I can only wonder at how many pieces of silver were your consulting fees.
>
> "Far more serious for my personal faith is the fact I must now decide if the Catholic Church has indeed succumbed to the attack of modernism and been corrupted in such a way to have been abandoned by God. I must now seriously consider if the branch of the church to which Gibson's family is a member is the one true Church...
>
> "May the good Lord have mercy on your souls."

And then this afterthought:

> "PS. Just so you know, I'm not a 70 year-old traditionalist, I am a 23 year-old recent college grad—I am the future" *(Boys 2003).*

oo0oo

Let me stay with Gibson's film a bit longer.
Mary Boys, one of the Catholic scholars who commented on the script, after seeing the film, wrote:

> "Having seen *The Passion of the Christ* when it debuted... I have no doubt that Gibson has substantially magnified the culpability of Jews at the expense of fidelity to gospel accounts. With few Jewish antagonists in this Passion drama, most notably Caiaphas and the Sanhedrin, are obsessed with brutalizing Jesus... *(Boys 2003)*

And this comment which is very relevant to today's biblical story:

> "Moreover, the power dynamics of Roman rule in Judea are reversed. The film portrays Pontius Pilate—whom history has revealed to be a venal and violent despot—as a contemplative philosopher who delicately weighs the nature of truth in conversations with his wife and, in the end, reluctantly orders

Jesus' death chiefly out of concern that Caiaphas will lead a revolt against him if he does not. Pilate and his wife Claudia... are the only characters in the film granted this level of complexity..."

*(Boys 2003)*

Pilate, historians say, ruled with an iron fist over every aspect of the province.
The military. The courts. The economy.
And even the Jewish Temple.

Jewish historian Philo paints a dark picture of a ruthless despot:

> 'by nature rigid and stubbornly harsh... of spiteful disposition and an exceeding wrathful man... the bribes, the acts of violence, the outrages, the cases of spiteful treatment, the constant murders without trial, the ceaseless and most grievous brutality'.

John is not an historian. He's a storyteller. Even a theologian.
If such an event as the trial ever took place,
Pilate's only concern would be simple:
is this person a harmless religious dreamer,
or a dangerous insurrectionist.

So why does John tell this story the way he does?
For several reasons I guess, but I reckon, for at least this important reason.
Jesus/Yeshua was not brought down by atheism and anarchy.
He was brought down by law and order politics, allied with religion!

And that has an old, but very modern, ring to it.

oo0oo

John has told his story. But it is not a unique story.
Sons and daughters of God have been killed throughout history.
As one commentator has pointed out:

> 'They have been killed in holy wars and inquisitions, concentration camps and prison cells. They have been killed in Cape Town, Memphis, El Salvador and Alabama. The charges against them have run the gamut, but treason and blasphemy have headed the list...'

When John has Jesus saying his 'reign was not of this world',
he did not suggest that was in some otherworldly 'left behind' place.
Jesus continually invited people to live lives of
justice and compassion,
understanding and generosity.
To re-imagine this world.

And this invitation, this reign, was given expression by others, back then,
in that collection of sayings we now call the 'Beatitudes'.

Today it is being given expression in remembering
the lives of thousands from El Salvador.

On 16 November 1989, six Jesuits and two women were murdered
in El Salvador at the Jesuit University
for speaking up and acting for justice.

They were killed by soldiers trained at the US Army School of Americas
in Fort Benning, Georgia.
In the years before and after, over 70,000 men, women and children
were killed in the violence and struggle for justice in El Salvador.

Last weekend, thousands of people gathered at the gates of Fort Benning
to protest the continued existence of this school, now called the
Western Hemisphere Institute for Security Co-operation.

To my mind, it is in the actions of those who gathered at the gates,
rather than those who gathering in the cinemas,
who have the more legitimate claim
to be honouring and celebrating the Reign of Christ.

Because what we believe about life and faith, can make a huge difference to us.
May it be so with you and me.

**Notes:**

Boys, M. C. An article on The Passion of The Christ in *Cross Currents* (2003) and Accessed through The Text This Week web site. http://www.textweek.com/. 2006.

# Pluralism is Not Some Religious 'Fruit Salad'

Pluralism Sunday, 2011

"Every religious tradition on earth has… developed in interaction
with others; not in isolation, in some watertight compartment…
The Christian idea of God has been a part of the world history
of the idea of God on earth, Christians receiving from, contributing to
and participating in that total history…
We have all along been participants
in the world history of religion; although we did not know it"
*(W. C. Smith)*

In an overseas poll about 10 years ago a cross section of citizens
were asked a series of questions to measure
the acceptance of religious pluralism *(Borg 2003).*

• To the question:
'Should Christians seek to convert people of other faiths
or leave them alone?'
22 per cent said 'convert';
71 per cent said 'leave them alone'.

• To the statement:
'All religions have elements of truth'.
78 per cent said 'yes'.

• To the statement:
'My religion is the only true religion'.
17 per cent said 'yes'.

Today, in progressive church circles, is Pluralism Sunday.
A day to give thanks for religious diversity.

To commit ourselves to a deepened sense of and respect for
human diversity and pluralism. And to appreciate more fully
"the richness of meaning and value which these diverse forms of
life have opened up for human beings" *(Kaufman 1996: 132).*

As it has been pointed out by many, both biblical and theological scholars have known for a long time that no religious idea or scripture text
can be properly or fully grasped simply by itself.

"Texts and ideas", writes former Harvard theologian Gordon Kaufman,
"can be understood only if we… see them in the context of other ideas and texts to which they are related and with which they are interconnected" *(Kaufman 1996: 133).*

Despite these somewhat academic sounding words, we already know this.
We are a part of the 'web of life'.
We live in a 'global village'.

What happens in one part of the world,
be it economical, political, or to do with the environment,
has its effects on all of us.

"We breathe a common atmosphere", says Kaufman,"and we all suffer from its growing pollution. We live together under the threat of nuclear and ecological disaster" *(Kaufman 1996:133).*

And again:

"Although culturally we are increasingly aware both of our diversity and of our interdependence, the meaning of this for our religious institutions and traditions, and for our religious self-understanding, has barely begun to dawn upon us"
*(Kaufman 1996: 133).*

So how could we respond?
Well, for one, we need new and more adequate ways
to think both the diversity
and the interconnectedness of our human religiousness.

Especially if our religious traditions are to be a positive contributor
to building a world in which, with all our differences,
we can live productively and in peace.

Which is why, in progressive church circles around the world,
today is Pluralism Sunday.

oo0oo

In 1788 when the First Fleet arrived on these shores from England,
Governor Arthur Phillip not only established a penal colony,
a gaol for the 736 convicts and to a certain extent,
the marines and officers who accompanied them,
it has also been said he won the land for 'protestant' Christianity
*(Breward 1988: 2).*

However, instead of that experience being a search for a feeling
of reconnection to a healthy kind of wholeness, Phillip saw religion as a
"useful package of warnings and admonitions that supplemented
the cell, chains, the lash, the gallows, or the rewards and remissions
for good conduct" *(Blainey 1987: 429).*

Hence Christianity was in the main rejected by the convicts
and only slightly embraced by the free settlers in latter years.

Which has led some to conclude that in Australia,
Christianity has always been rather a casual affair.
And at best, the nation was only ever superficially christianised
*(Wilson 1982: 6).*

But this hasn't stopped many fundamentalists today
from claiming: 'Jesus is the ONLY doorway'.

Indeed, one such tract—No. 151 it said, and free 'as the Lord provides'—
was placed in my letter box a few days ago. The second in as many days.
I think 'Pastor Peter' from wherever, is trying to tell me something!

A far more honest and open response comes from
New Zealander, Sir Lloyd Geering.
In one of his recent books, *Coming Back To Earth,* he writes:

"Humans show themselves to be religious whenever and wherever they take the questions of human existence seriously, and then create a common response to whatever they find to be of ultimate value to them… With but rare exceptions, people everywhere and at all times have made some kind of response to the demands of human existence. They have tried to make something of life. They have looked for meaning and purpose. They have hoped for some kind of fulfillment"*(Geering 2008: 151).*

And this is true even though an increasing number of us
have grown dissatisfied with the religious forms and theologies of the past.
'Why weren't we told?' is a common lament.

As one of my progressive colleagues has suggested:
We don't want our religion in the old way.
We cannot give up our minds for it.
We cannot become pre-modern people.
We are not interested in being saved from or saving others from hell in the afterlife.
We are not interested in converting people to our religion or in proving that our book is of divine origin.

Taking all this with radical seriousness, Geering suggests the characteristics of a contemporary spirituality are likely to include:

- An attitude of awe towards this self-evolving universe.
- An appreciation of the living ecosphere of this planet.
- An appreciation of the capacity of the earth to regenerate itself.
- An appreciation of the total cultural legacy we have received from our human forbears.
- Responsibility for the care of one another.
- Responsibility for the kind of planet we pass on to our descendants.
- Its value to be found in life, in all of its diversity.

He goes on:

> "In developing a spirituality for today's secular world we must not be primarily concerned with saving our individual selves... Rather we must be primarily concerned for the welfare of one another, for the future of the human species, and for the health of the planet" *(Geering 2008: 201).*

Sentiments also expressed in Susan Griffin's eco-feminist poem *Woman and Nature*:

This earth is my sister;
I love her daily grace,
her silent daring,
and how loved I am
*How we admire this strength in each other,*
*all that we have lost,*

*all that we have suffered,*
*all that we know:*
*we are stunned by this beauty,*
and I do not forget;
what she is to me,
what I am to her *(Quoted in Christ 2003:239-40).*

Which is why, in progressive church circles around the world,
today is Pluralism Sunday.

oo0oo

First celebrated in 2007, Pluralism Sunday is now as then, sponsored by The Center for Progressive Christianity, in the USA.

Indeed, as part of its Eight (8) Points detailing an understanding of what it means to be 'progressive', TCPC has as its Second point:

> *Recognize the faithfulness of other people who have other names for the way to God's realm, and acknowledge that their ways are true for them, as our ways are true for us.*

Pluralism is not some religious 'fruit salad' where anything goes.
It is about embracing other religions and honouring them
at a deep level of respect and openness.

And Pluralism Sunday is about letting the world of newspaper columnists
and TV producers and the neighbours
with whom you chat over the back fence,
know there are Christian pluralistic churches out there
who challenge the exclusive dogmatism of the fundamentalist churches
and their claim that Christianity is religiously superior.

There is a way to be authentically and particularly religious,
involved and immersed in a religious culture, and
practice a specific religion and path, but…

> "if you go all the way with that, you will discover that we all end up on the top of the same mountain [with]… brothers and sisters of other faiths who have done the same sort of thing" *(Burklo, 2007).*

**Notes:**

Blainey, G. "Sydney 1877" in (ed) D. J. Mulvaney, J. P. White. *Australians. To 1788*. Broadway: Fairfax, Syme and Weldon Associates, 1987.
Borg, M. J. *The Heart Of Christianity. Rediscovering A Life Of Faith*. New York: HarperSanFrancisco, 2003.
Breward, I. *Australia. The Most Godless Place Under Heaven*. Mitcham: Beacon Hill Books, 1988.
Burklo, J. A sermon. The Center for Progressive Christianity web site. Accessed March 2007.
Christ, C. P. *She Who Changes. Re-imagining The Divine In The World*. New York: Palgrave/Macmillan, 2003.
Geering, L. G. *Coming Back To Earth: From Gods, To God, To Gaia*. Santa Rosa: Polebridge Press, 2008.
Kaufman, G. D. *God, Mystery, Diversity. Christian Theology In A Pluralistic World*. Minneapolis: Fortress Press, 1996.
Shuck, J. "Sermon". Shuck & Jive blog site, 2010. Accessed March 2011.
Smith, W. C. *Towards A World Theology*. Philadelphia: Westminster Press, 1981.
Wilson, B. "The church in a secular society" in D. Harris, D. Hynd, D. Millikan. (ed) *The Shape Of Belief. Christianity In Australia Today*. Homebush: Lancer Books, 1982.

# The Earth that We Knew… is Gone. Long Live Eaarth!

Season of Creation 1, 2010
Theme: Ocean

"The Copenhagen conference, in December 2009, was supposed to be the place where the world took an 'historic step forward'. Instead, it turned into a fiasco of the first order"
*(Bill McKibben).*

We are living in a scientific, pluralistic age.
And unless you have been living under a cabbage leaf,
then you will also be aware of the current universal debates about how

> "our modern life-style is harming other creatures, diminishing the functioning of ecosystems, and altering our global climate patterns
> *(Peters 2002:viii).*

Planet Earth is in peril. All creation is suffering.
As you can imagine or already know, several folk have put their concerns
in books,
during workshops,
at politically rallies and conferences, and
through the media.

And as I have for the past five years, today's liturgy, and the ones
for the next three weeks, all follow an added new Lectionary season…
The Season of Creation.

Much of the impetus for this new liturgical season comes from
the work of Australian 'progressive' scholar, Norman Habel.

Traditionally the church calendar or Lectionary is shaped around three years.
And each year has seven main seasons:
Advent, Christmas, Epiphany,
Easter, Pentecost, Lent.
And then the rather long general time called After Pentecost or
Ordinary Sundays.

This additional season claims some of that After Pentecost time
by designating the four Sundays in September each year,
traditionally associated with Spring in the southern hemisphere,
as the Season of Creation.

And each of those four days has been given a theme.
This year the themes are Ocean, Fauna, Storm, and Cosmos.
So I would like to think it is important stuff
we are saying and doing this morning.

oo0oo

I am informed that approximately 71% of the earth's surface
is covered by ocean—a continuous body of water that is
customarily divided into several principal oceans and smaller seas.

More than half of this area is over 3,000 metres in depth.
And the collective volume is approximately 1.3 billion cubic kilometres.
The deepest part is in the Northern Mariana Trench,
10,923 meters deep, in the Pacific Ocean.

Scientists also claim that life within the ocean evolved some
three (3) billion years prior to life on land.
And they estimate that 230,000 marine life-forms of all types
are currently known, but the total could be
up to 10 times that number.

We also know that the ocean has a significant effect on the biosphere.
Oceanic evaporation as a phase of the water cycle,
is the source of most rainfall and ocean temperatures
determine both climate and wind patterns that affect life on land.

But… the oceans, the sea, that 71% of the earth's surface
we usually don't consider much outside our Summer vacations,
is changing due to global warming.

Now, as I was preparing these comments
a few things were happening around me:

(i) I was reading Bill McKibben's latest book,
*Eaarth: Making A Life On A Tough New Planet.*
My reading was primarily to do a book review
for the State denominational magazine.

(ii) The BP oil slick in the Gulf of Mexico was continuing to grow,
and all attempts to stem its flow were proving to be in vain.

Indeed, in a radio interview on ABC Radio National Breakfast,
McKibben said that this year we will really sense God's humour
when the hurricane season strikes…
• they will go further inland and live longer, due to the sun's rays being absorbed by the dark surface of the oil, warming the air, dropping even more record rain.

And while that interview was happening…
(iii) Reports were coming in a water spout had crossed the coastline
in far northern New South Wales causing extensive damage.
Callers to ABC North Coast radio reported there had been falls
of more than 270 millimetres (nearly 11 inches) of rain that morning.

So the theme of Ocean Sunday was suddenly proving to be very important.

oo0oo

Bill McKibben is an author and founder of the environmental organizations
*Step It Up* and *350.org* and was one of the first to warn
of the dangers of global warming.

I invite you to listen to a selection of just some of Bill McKibben's
comments on oceans and climate warming:

> "The oceans… are distinctly more acid and their level is rising;
> they are also warmer, which means the greatest storms of our
> planet, hurricanes and cyclones, have become more powerful"
> *(McKibben 2010:45)*

How come?
Because of our emissions and our burning of cheap fossil fuel, a process "that Britain's Royal Society described as 'essentially irreversible'" *(McKibben 2010:10).*

To make his point further McKibben says:

> "One barrel of oil yields as much energy as 25,000 hours of human manual labor—more than a decade of human labor per barrel. The average American uses 25 barrels each year, which is like finding 300 years of free labor annually. And that's just the oil; there's coal and gas, too" *(McKibben 2010:27).*

Economics and growth have become the watchwords for modernity!

At the same time research is showing the earth's ice caps and glaciers are melting with "disconcerting and unexpected speed" *(McKibben 2010:45).*

We have already raised the temperature nearly a degree Celsius.

McKibben continues:

> "...the ocean is more acid than anytime in the last eight hundred thousand years, and at current rates by 2050 it will be more corrosive than anytime in the past 20 million years" *(McKibben 2010:10).*

And again:

> "On the last day of 2008, the *Economist* reported that temperatures on the Antarctic Peninsula were rising faster than anywhere else on earth, and that the West Antarctic was losing ice 75 percent faster than just a decade before.... Name a major feature of the earth's surface and you'll find massive change" *(McKibben 2010:5).*

The changes could hardly be more fundamental!

> "The earth that we knew—the only earth that we ever knew—is gone" *(McKibben 2010:27).*

oo0oo

If you are beginning to hear 'doomsday' and 'apocalypse'
then I guess I can't blame you.
I had similar feelings as I read McKibben's book.

We can be numbed by all the figures and percentages.
We can say the scientists are probably overstating our woes.
The anticipated future can be paralysed by our fears.

Indeed, it's hard to brace ourselves

> "for the jump to a new world when we still, kind of, live in the old one... We're so used to *growth* that we can't imagine alternatives; at best we embrace the squishy *sustainable*, with its implied claim that we can keep on as before" *(McKibben 2010:102).*

Well, McKibben is not all negative and alarmist.
He does offer some suggestions—some words or metaphors—for change.
And those five words are: Durable, Sturdy, Stable, Hardy, Robust.

For us that means reshaping our society:
• from big to smaller,
• from growth to maintenance,
• from expansion to scale down,
• from global to neighbourhood.
But to get the full gist of his arguments you'll have to read his book!

oo0oo

Human beings, especially in the so-called 'West', have historically been reluctant to consider themselves as part of the web of nature.
Indeed a web within a web.

Likewise, Australia does not have a good record
when it comes to climate change.

Governments since the early 1990s have all adopted a strategy
of more-or-less do little to nothing at home
and work hard to prevent others from taking major action.

So there has been an encouragement of community apathy.

Not to mention the often cosy relationships between the fossil-fuel
lobbyists, called the 'greenhouse mafia', and many politicians,
all exposed by a 2006 ABC TV *Four Corners* program, and
Clive Hamilton's book, *Scorcher: The Dirty Politics of Climate Change.*

But if our biblical tradition suggests anything, human beings are part of nature.
The problems comes when Christians—usually fundamentalists—
claim that the mythical stories of Genesis 1 and 2,
are more 'true' or more 'factual' than science and evolution.

So in many quarters there is a raging attack on 'progressive' religion:
• from fundamentalists who don't believe one can accept evolution
and be religious, and
• from the 'new atheists' who caricature all people of religion
as fundamentalists *(MZimmerman).*

But modern science and progressive theology are saying
and have been saying, again and again:
the universe must be regarded as a whole;
it is of intrinsic value, and each part,
participates in that intrinsic value as each part
participates in this wonderful web of life.

Each part… rather than one species or organism
separating itself out as more important than the rest.

It is time for radical change. It is urgent.
To recall the words of a past long-haired, locust eating, desert prophet:
'The axe is at the root of the tree.'

Global warming is not just another important issue
that human beings need to deal with.
Rather, it is the demand that we live differently.
And it demands a paradigm shift in who we think we are
*(McFague 2008:44).*

So we do something important today.
As we begin the season of Spring we also begin to celebrate
the liturgical Season of Creation.

And to be reminded we are a part of nature,
even as the oceans, the fauna, the storm and the cosmos, are.

A part of nature. A part of the universe. That whole
"complex, interrelated and interacting... matter-energy in space-time... of which humans are an integral part..." *(Gillett 2006:1).*

**Notes:**

Gillett, P. R. "Theology of, by, and for religious naturalism" in *Journal Of Liberal Religion* 6, 1, 1-6. (An online journal), 2006.

Hamilton, C. *Scorcher: The Dirty Politics Of Climate Change***.** Melbourne: Black Inc., 2007.

McFague, S. *A New Climate For Theology. God, The World, And Global Warming*. Minneapolis: Fortress Press, 2008.

McKibben, Bill. *Eaarth: Making A Life On A Tough New Planet.* Melbourne: Black Inc. 2010.

Peters, K. E. *Dancing With The Sacred. Evolution, Ecology, And God.* Harrisburg: Trinity Press International, 2002.

Zimmerman, M. "The Clergy Letter Project", In the *Huffington Post*, 22/5/2010.

# Coming Home to the Cosmos

Season of Creation 4, 2010
Theme: Cosmos

"Everything in the universe is related.
Can you feel that umbilical cord to the Cosmos?
Can you feel the strands of connectedness—the interpendent web—of all existence, even with all human beings?"
*(DeWolf 2008).*

Bruce Sanguin, the Canadian author and
progressive minister in Vancouver,
has written and important book called
*Darwin, Divinity, And The Dance Of The Cosmos.*
It is from this book I have borrowed the title of this sermon.

Today we celebrate the fourth Sunday in the new
Lectionary season called *Season of Creation.*
And the theme for this day is Cosmos Sunday,
hence the sermon title.

In the first chapter of his book, Sanguin tells of a time,
while still a theological student, he was in a café
eating an egg salad sandwich and reading a poem.

The poem so affected him he said it felt as if
"someone had peeled back a layer of reality to reveal the invisible radiance of what lay behind and within all creation" *(Sanguin 2007:20).*

Let me share that poem, published in his book:
This sunset…
This smile…
This word you are writing…
This pain you are feeling…
The question you are asking…
This omelette you are cooking…

The meaning of life
is the tear of joy
shed at the
sight of
the
well-cooked omelette *(JPramuk).*

Reflecting on his experience, Sanguin says:

> "If the poem I read expressed any truth at all, it was this: if we could truly see what is before our eyes, day in and day out, the sacred radiance of creation would drop us to our knees and render us speechless. We would know ourselves to be in as much divine presence as we can handle in this earthly realm" *(Sanguin 2007:21-22).*

Today, Cosmos Sunday, is an invitation to once again feel deeply and organically connected with planet Earth.

Today, Cosmos Sunday, is also an invitation for the Church to 'get with' a 21st century cosmology…

> "There is a new story of creation, which needs to inform our biblical stories of creation… [And this new evolutionary cosmological story] simply cannot be contained by old models and images of God, and outmoded ways of being the church" *(Sanguin 2007:27-28).*

oo0oo

In every age the worlds of theology and religion interact with the cultural and scientific worldviews of that day.
Such interaction between the two is essential
"to make religious faith both credible and relevant within a
particular generation's view of the world and how it works"
*(Johnson 2007:286).*

Sharing Sanguin's concern, feminist Catholic theologian Elizabeth Johnson says:
"In sum, theological reflection today should endeavor to speak

about God's relation not to an ancient nor medieval nor Newtonian
world, but to the dynamic, emergent, self-organizing universe
that contemporary natural and biological sciences describe"
*(Johnson 2007:287).*

Scientists tell us the 'Great Story' as we understand it today, begins with the ultimate mystery of the Big Bang, some 13.7 billion years ago.
Life on Earth originated some four billion years ago.
*Homo habilis* (our ancestors) begin using tools 2.5 million years ago.
Symbolic language emerges between 50,000 and 500,000 years ago.
Classical religions emerge around 3,000-4,000 years ago.
I emerged just over 66 years ago.

Billions of years of cosmic evolution have produced us.
The ancestral stars are a part of our genealogy.

"Out of the stars in their flight,
out of the dust of eternity, here have we come,
Stardust and sunlight, mingling
through time and through space" *(Weston 1993).*

If we put our 13.7 billion year universe on a clock of one hour,
"humanity appears in only the last few seconds" *(Peters 2002:127).*

The sheer immensity of the cosmos
is very hard to get one's head around.

The fragments of knowledge we do have, suggest:
• one million bodies the size of Earth can fit in the volume of the Sun;
• each star has a sun;
• there are 100,000 million stars in the Milky Way galaxy;
• there are approx. 100,000 million galaxies;
• it has taken light 12,000 million years to reach us from the farthest reaches of space;
• the current diameter of the observable cosmos/universe is thought to be about 93 billion light years.

It is absolutely essential to make religious faith both credible and relevant within a particular generation's view of the world and how it works!

oo0oo

In light of all this let me offer a couple of additional comments, from
(i) a professor of the History of Ideas, and an atheist, and
(ii) a professor of Philosophy and Religion, and a religious naturalist.
I invite you to ponder them sometime.

(i) Ronald Aronson reminds us that the sights and sounds that delight us are determined by the sun.

The sun is near enough to Earth but not too near,
far enough from it but not too far.

"Green leaves as far as the eye can see are part of the life-sustaining process of photosynthesis, which uses the sunlight, carbon dioxide, and water to create both the energy that fuels living things and the oxygen of the atmosphere. We dwell in and breathe the oxygen, are made of water and Earth's other elements, and consume living things in order to survive, as they do each other. But all this happens only because we all possess the very same chemical, physical, and biological structures" *(Aronson 2008:46-47).*

We all possess the very same chemical, physical, and biological structures…
Mmm.

While (ii) Karl Peters confirms that nature is in us
as much as we are in nature.

"We are webs of reality, woven out of the threads of culture, biology, and the cosmos according to recipes (structures of language and values, DNA codes, and laws of nature) in each. As webs of reality each of us is a manifestation of a large part of the universe as a whole" *(Peters 1992:412).*

These comments plus many others, go to the core of our beliefs:
How can we now describe the experience we call G-o-d?

Traditionally it seems, most Christians have imagined God
as The Creator, a kind of supernatural person-like reality
who has brought everything into being.

However all that is now changing.
New religious stories or myths are being shaped.

Stories which understand the presence of G-o-d that is compatible with the ideas of modern science.

And the new story which I find personally compelling is experiencing and understanding G-o-d

> "as simply the creativity that has brought forth the world and all its contents, from the Big Bang all the way down to the present"
> *(Kaufman 2006:xi).*

Former Harvard theologian, Gordon Kaufman, has said:

> "Imagining God as creativity enables Christian thinkers to be much more attuned to what the modern sciences have been teaching us about our lives and the world in which we live. It makes it possible to bridge the divide often felt between religious faith and our scientific knowledge" *(Kaufman 2006:xi).*

So, what might it mean to be progressively religious in the 21st century? Some of my responses include:

- To be progressively religious in the 21st century is to see ourselves "as webs of cosmos, life, and culture, so that we and the rest of our planet can continue and flourish" *(Peters 2002:136)*...
- To be progressively religious in the 21st century is to be devoted to maximising the future of the earth and all living creatures whose destiny is increasingly in our hands...
- To be progressively religious in the 21st century is to value the importance of the human relationships which bind us together into social groups...
- To be progressively religious in the 21st century is to place the needs of the global society before those of our own immediate family, tribe or nation... *(Geering 1998:46)*
- To be progressively religious in the 21st century is to celebrate life.

Such a 21st century progressive religion is also, I want to suggest, a response to the vision and efforts and the life of

> the Galilean sage we call Jesus/Yeshua, without the baggage of christological beliefs unnecessarily added by the church
> *(Wink 2000:177).*

So where are we...

(i) If we put all this together the new Great Story suggests the whole universe is alive and changing, continually co-creating new possibilities of life.

Change **is**!
Or remembering the ground-breaking work of Charles Darwin published 150 years ago, change is the core of

cosmic evolution,
biological evolution,
cultural evolution

(ii) The word 'environment' literally means "that which surround us". So if we were actually to notice that which surround us, then

> "[a]t the very least, we would ***notice*** changes in the seasonal flights of birds. We would ***notice*** if the mosquito population doubled or tripled. We would ***notice*** if more and more trees had dead limbs. Instead of reading about the effects of global warming, we would ***notice*** them in our daily experience!" *(Hill 2008: 68).*

As contemporary progressive theology reminds us time and time again,

G-o-d or the Sacred or Creativity does not reside in some other place called 'heaven'. Nor is heaven our goal.

The world is our true home. Indeed, our only home.

> "This life is meant to be enjoyed. To enjoy life is to cherish the beauty of each living thing, to be interested in diversity and difference in the web of life..." *(Christ 2003:116).*

May the story of the ones who discovered the whole cosmos/universe/planet as alive and changing, continually, and

that novelty and surprise makes life interesting... *(Christ 2003:171).*
always awaken within us new possibilities for the now.

**Notes:**


Aronson, R. *Living Without God: New Directions For Atheists, Agnostics, Secularists, And The Undecided*. Berkley: Counterpoint, 2008.

Ayala, F. J. "The evolution of life: An overview" in M. K. Cunningham (ed) *God And Evolution. A Reader*. Oxon: Routledge, 2007.

Birch, L. C. *Nature And God*. London: SCM Press, 1965.

Christ, C. P. *She Who Changes. Re-imagining The Divine In The World*. New York: PalgraveMacmillan, 2003.

DeWolf, M. L. "What do we mean – 'Thank God for evolution'?" Nature Coast Unitarian Universalists Church, 2008. The ClergyLetter Project web site. Accessed February 2009.

Geering, L. *Does Society Need Religion?* Wellington: St Andrew's Trust for the Study of Religion and Society, 1998.

Hill, J. A. *Ethics In The Global Village. Moral Insights For The Post 9-11 USA*. Santa Rosa: Polebridge Press, 2008.

Johnson, E. A. "Does God play dice? Divine providence and chance" in M. K. Cunningham (ed) *God And Evolution. A Reader*. Oxon: Routledge, 2007.

Kaufman, G. D. *Jesus And Creativity*. Minneapolis: Augsburg Fortress, 2006.

———————. *In the Beginning… Creativity*. Minneapolis: Fortress Press, 2004.

Peters, K. E. *Dancing With The Sacred. Evolution, Ecology, and God*. Harrisburg: Trinity International, 2002.

——————— "Interrelating nature, humanity, and the work of God: Some issues for future reflection" in *Zygon: Journal Of Religion & Science 27*, 4, 403-419. 1992.

Sanguin, B. *Darwin, Divinity, And The Dance Of The Cosmos. An Ecological Christianity*. Kelowna: CopperHouse/Wood Lake Publishing, 2007.

Weston, R. T. "Out of the stars" in 530/*Singing The Living Tradition*. Boston: Beacon Press/UUA, 1993.

Wink, W. "The Son of Man the stone that builders rejected" in R. Funk/ Jesus Seminar. *The Once And Future Jesus*. Santa Rosa: Polebridge Press, 2000.

# Afterword

## Against the Stream, While Continuing the Journey

Mark 5:21-43

As you would all know, this is my last sermon as minister in this place.
And who knows, as I move into retirement, it just might be my last!
I am also aware some of you are here this morning because of this event.
Thank you. I am most grateful and honoured by your presence.

I have also been told I had better make this sermon a good one!
Well… I have thought long and hard about what I should say.
And having discussed the matter with the 'Worship-in-the-Round' folk,
we have decided I should speak on the church's two favourite
subjects: 'sex' and 'alcohol'.
We reckoned they might be two sure-fire winners!
Well… if not those issues, perhaps something equally as human.

oo0oo

"Should I touch him?
The pain of stretching.
Pushing my way through.
Touching.
Touching just his dangling tassel.
No one will know.
No one needs to know…
No one knows what I've been through.
No one knows the shame..." *(Loader 2003).*

So begins a poetic reflection on today's gospel story
by West Australian New Testament scholar, William (Bill) Loader.
You will recall I have often quoted Bill's thoughts and comments

over the past nine years, even when I reckon
he could have been more 'progressive' than he really was.

But back to his reflection…
A reflection which touches the pain of the story.
A story which touches a woman's pain of living with loss.
The loss of health.
The loss of respect.
The loss of intimacy.
The loss of social standing and her place in the community.

Throughout many years, or at least, for as long as her money had lasted,
the woman has repeatedly explored every possibility
of obtaining relief from her embarrassing and isolating complaint.

> "It is… with the desperation born of this wearisome history, that
> the woman now clutches at the straw which Jesus' presence affords"
> *(Cairns 2004:70).*

When we are pushed to our limit, we will do anything
to find relief or help for ourselves, and for those whom we love.
Even if it means breaking social and religious taboos.
Even if it means sailing from Indonesia or Sri Lanka to Australia
in an old, leaky, wooden boat.

oo0oo

The woman with the haemorrhage (permanent menstruation),
a seemingly hopeless situation, knows what it is like
to be pushed to the limits—physically, emotionally, and of her resources.
"Doctors of the body merely aggravated her suffering" *(Carroll 2007: 48).*

Yet, as I am reminded by a not-so-progressive Melbourne
New Testament lecturer:

> "She is not a timid character, but extraordinarily courageous. By being present in the crowd and by touching Jesus, she is taking a great risk. She steals her healing because she is not free for it openly…" *(Lee 1993: 66).*

Pushing her way through the crowd she touches Jesus.
And a power, a wholeness, shaped by a profound
"sensitivity which is finely attuned to the feelings and emotions of the people around him" *(Cairns 2004:71)*
rather than any supernatural insight, transforms her life.

Her "intuitive trust" *(Carroll 2007:49)* is acknowledged.
Her dignity and respect are restored.

oo0oo

I am not unmindful that today, this set Lectionary reading
should be about two women:

- one 12 years young, perhaps surrounded by a caring family;
- one ill, disabled, a living death for 12 years, all alone.

Both marginalised because of their gender.

Not unmindful… also, that I am male.
But mindful of the role many males have had during my 40+ years of ministry.
And the irony of these stories about women and the 'power of faith',
compared to last weeks 'storm' story, about a
group of male disciples and the 'power of fear'.

Male disciples who were afraid of themselves.
Who had lost their courage.
Who experienced the storm not as challenge, but as evil threat...

By contrast the older woman in this week's story, acts courageously.
She claims her health. Her trust or faith
is in the pre-eminence of wellbeing
"over the forces that diminish and detract from life…" *(Cairns 2004:71).*

oo0oo

Mark the anonymous storyteller has shaped this story
to meet his community's need.
A need to be empowered by a renewed vision
of the 'realm of God'.

And he uses stories and imagination to do just that.

After a bit of reflection I also want to claim there have been people and issues, stories and imagination, challenge and wilderness, collectively,
who have also embraced and empowered my 40+ years in ministry.

At times the response to new initiatives and change has been warm and positive. At other times I copped a bollocking as I irritated the presumptions of my critics.
Both in the car park after meetings or a service,
and in church magazines following views expressed.

On all those occasions I declined to be intimidated by their bullying tactics, emotional blackmail, or threatened withdrawal of financial support.
To a fault, I have never tolerated fools easily!

Ralph Waldo Emerson expressed it well, I reckon, when he said:
'Do not be timid and squeamish. All of life is an experiment.
The more experiments you make, the better.'

Or as this 1960's Argus pop-poster, which used to be on my study wall in Wendouree (Victoria), my first parish, says:
"Behold the turtle who makes progress only when he sticks his neck out" *(CParker).*

Some of my personal 'church-type' experiences over the years have included:

- the establishment within the UCA Assembly of a national office of communications, followed by a National Communications Group;
- being ordered off a bus at gun point, in Suva, while on assignment with the Fijian Council of Churches, when I was caught taking photos during the first army coup;
- fighting bushfires, and later being part of the Uniting Church counselling team, as I was sent into the fire ravaged areas of the Western District of Victoria after Ash Wednesday 1983;
- meeting with young workers in South Korea after they had been attacked with broken bricks by the bosses 'thugs', because they were protesting for a fair wage;
- the founding of The Network of Biblical Storytellers, Australia/ New Zealand, as well as being a founding member of

the Provisional Council of the Wellspring Community: An Australian Community inspired by Iona in Scotland;
- the exacting work at Hobart Royal Hospital when, as Senior Uniting Church chaplain, I was part of a larger team supporting victims, survivors, and the accused, of the Port Arthur massacre.

While other experiences have seen both Dylis and I involved in:
- establishing playgroups, an infant welfare clinic, and 'meals on wheels' as a congregational response to growing, community needs;
- grief counselling, and the commencement of a branch of Do-Care for the elderly and shut-ins;
- the planning of Court Support with the Tasmanian Attorney General, for families prior to the proposed trial in the aftermath of Port Arthur; while
- Dylis has made two sets of liturgical banners—in Hobart and Canberra — as well as gifting me with my Albs and contemporary Aboriginal desert-design mono-stoles.

And the one or two things overseen here in Canberra, including:
- the re-development of part of this St James property,
- the crafting of both the Inclusive Tapestry and the Sanctuary Quilt, and
- the establishment of the important separate, but parallel, Centre for Progressive Religious Thought, which has helped organise the progressive or 'emergent' religion movement in Australia, and incidentally, put St James on the 'national map'.

"Against the stream"—a phrase from my early theology mentor Henry Nelson Wieman, has been a personal motto, as I have sought to counter the 'dumbing down' of religion and biblical literacy.

Hence, to re-imagine, reconceive and reconstruct, rather than just restate.

Several people have travelled with me on my theological journeys. Those whose thought I have encountered in books and web sites. Especially those deemed by others to be 'heretics'!

And those whom I have had the privilege of engaging with personally:

Brandon Scott, Val Webb, Lloyd Geering, Andrew Pratt, Jack Spong, Arthur Waskow, Gregory Jenks, Gretta Vosper, Ian Lawton, John Shuck, Bruce Sanguin, Nigel Leaves, Fred Plumer, and many others.

While much of my energy has been taken up by communication/social ecology and theology, a renewed interest in critical biblical scholarship was awakened 20+ years ago, when I encountered the exciting work of the Westar Institute and its famous (or infamous) 'Jesus Seminar'.

As an Associate colleague has said, the Jesus Seminar's work on the 'historical Jesus' has been very important because:

(i) it publicly tells a family secret, in a loud voice, in order to encourage open dialog about the scriptures, and

(ii) it models a collegial rather than an hierarchical way of operating *(Schweitzer-Mordecai 2007:66).*

As neither are the accepted processes of the existing church systems, its actions are a threat *(Schweitzer-Mordecai 2007:70)* as can be seen and experienced in nearly every Uniting Church theological college today.

All of you:

- those who are part of this congregation called St James, a rainbow of Uniting, Catholic, Anglican, Lutheran, Baptist, Assembly of God, 'church alumni', Home church, Greek Orthodox; young and older, abled and differently abled, gay and straight;
- those of you who have been part of other congregations and placements and community groups along the way, in Victoria, NSW, and Tasmania;
- those of you who have joined me in the 'progressive religion movement', especially through the Common Dreams Conferences;
- those of you who have regularly visited my web site, and offered encouraging and grateful comments… and
- not forgetting those important and loving people called my family, you have all been part of this personal journey.

I regard myself as extremely fortunate that it was during the late 60s and early 70s which set the matrix for my theological and ministry formation.

For they were exciting days to be doing theology:

- post 'death-of-God' theology days,
- in the midst of 'process and empirical theology' days,

and before the return of conservative neo-orthodoxy
which has shackled the church ever since.

That conservative neo-orthodoxy wants to elevate the place of belief and creeds and the *Basis of Union*, into forms of control,
policing the 'boundaries of faith'.

That conservative neo-orthodoxy sees a broad, genuine, and open 'inclusiveness', as a threat to the viability of the church.

That conservative neo-orthodoxy is frightened of honest and serious scholarship, especially that seeking to discover the fragments of the vision
of the sage we call Jesus/Yeshua, dismissing it at times as
'deeply problematic' or 'troubling'; at other times
with insulting insinuations.

This fear is often palpable and has made parts of the Uniting Church an unsafe place for open biblical and theological scholarship,
outside their preferred 'square'.
No wonder church numbers are continuing to shrink
and progressive religion and the 'church alumni' are growing!

So the urgent question facing the church right now are:

- How long can we count on suspended disbelief to shore up our outworn religious myths? *(Hedrick 2004)*

oo0oo

Jesus' vision or myth of the 'realm of God', as we can sense it in the stories of the bloke we now call Mark,
and discovered in critical biblical scholarship, warts and all,
appears to have been one of inclusive wholeness.

It restored people's humanity and life.
It invited people to grasp new opportunities.
It drew people "on to a more authentic humanness" *(Kaufman 1993:308)*.

The 'historical' Jesus rather than the mythical Christ of faith and creed, can

"yet become the Jesus of the future by providing for us the model of that human wisdom which our age so desperately needs"
*(Geering 2000:145).*

So whether your response to Mark's story be 'faith' or 'fear'
will be in direct relationship to the way you view this sage called Jesus/Yeshua.
The choice is yours to make.

True, the old reality is tenacious.

Even with colleagues, and within committees and councils and fellowship groups in progressive congregations!
So to further the 'progressive' challenge, it will continue to need grassroots people of courage, imagination, and determination
to continue the journey.

Alas, too many progressives choose to remain silent,
seemingly afraid to use the word 'progressive' to describe their stance.
That leaves them lying low, sitting quietly in their pews in church, or in meditation groups, or leaving altogether
and joining the 'church alumni'.

But in his day Rabbi Abraham Heschel, refused to let institutional religion off the hook. And neither should we!
In a collection of articles honouring his thought, Heschel reflected:

"It is customary to blame secular science and anti-religious philosophy for the eclipse of religion in modern society. It would be more honest to blame religion for its own defeats."

And then these telling words:

"Religion declined not because it was refuted, but because it became irrelevant, dull, oppressive, insipid. When faith is completely replaced by creed, worship by discipline; love by habit; when the crisis of today is ignored because of the splendor of the past; when faith becomes an heirloom rather than a living fountain; when religion speaks only in the name of authority rather than with the voice of compassion—its message becomes meaningless"
*(Fox 2004:426).*

As for me…? Well, as I begin to move into retirement from active service, I am initially attracted to some words by the Russian writer, Rozanov:

> "All religions will pass, but this will remain. Simply sitting in a chair, and looking in the distance" *(Holloway 2001).*

Only problem is, there are still many more things,
personal and collective, I wish to help shape.

Life's stages each have their own validity.
It is important to live as fully as possible.
For as long as we live, we continue to make ourselves.
Continuous evolution!
Ceaseless creativity!
So I look forward to all the new challenges and horizons
and sages along the way,
these next stages will disclose.

In the meantime, I wish you well as together and separately,
you continue in the spirit of the Jesus journey.
For me, it truly has been "a more adventurous life" *(Wieman 1928).*

**Notes:**


Cairns, I. J. *Mark Of A Non-realist. A Contemporary Reading Of The Second Gospel.* Masterton: Fraser Books, 2004.

Carroll, J. *The Existential Jesus.* Carlton North: Scribe Publications, 2007.

Geering, L. "The legacy of Christianity" in R. W. Funk/Jesus Seminar (ed) *The Once And Future Jesus.* Santa Rosa: Polebridge Press, 2000.

Hedrick, C. W. "The 'good news' about the historical Jesus" in A. Dewey. (ed) *The Historical Jesus Goes To Church.* Santa Rosa: Polebridge Press, 2004.

Holloway, R. *Doubts And Loves. What Is Left Of Christianity.* Edinburgh: Canongate Books, 2001.

Kaufman, G. D. *In Face Of Mystery. A Constructive Theology.* Cambridge: Harvard University Press, 1993.

Lee, D. A. & J Honner. (ed) *Wisdom And Demons. Meditations On Scripture.* Richmond: David Lovell Books, 1993.

Loader, W. "First Thoughts on Gospel Passages from the Lectionary". http: //wwwstaff.murdoch.edu.au/~loader/lectionaryindex.html, Accessed 2003.

Parker, C. "Behold the turtle…" Art Poster. Niles: Argus Communications.

Schweitzer-Mordecai, R. "The Jesus intervention" in B. B. Scott. (ed) *Jesus Reconsidered. Scholarship In The Public Eye.* Santa Rosa: Polebridge Press, 2007.

Wieman, H. N. *The Wrestle Of Religion With Truth.* New York: Macmillan Press, 1928.

# Further Reading


Borg, M. J. *Evolution Of The Word. The New Testament In The Order The Books Were Written*. New York: HarperCollins, 2012.

Crossan, J. D. *The Power Of Parable. How Fiction By Jesus Became Fiction About Jesus*. New York: HarperOne, 2012.

Cupitt, D. *A New Great Story*. Salem: Polebridge Press, 2010.

Felten, D. & J. Procter-Murphy. *Living The Questions. The Wisdom Of Progressive Christianity*. New York: HarperOne, 2012.

Freeman, C. *AD 381. Heretics, Pagans, And The Dawn Of The Monotheistic State*. Woodstock: The Overlook Press, 2008.

Geering, L. G. *Such Is Life. A Close Encounter With Ecclesiastes.* Wellington: Steele Roberts, 2010

Grigg, R. *Beyond The God Delusion. How Radical Theology Harmonizes Science And Religion*. Minneapolis: Fortress Press, 2008.

Habel, N. *Rainbow of Mysteries: Meeting the Sacred in Nature*. Kelowna: Wood Lake Publishers, 2012.

Jenks, G. C. *The Once And Future Bible. An Introduction To The Bible For Religious Progressives*. Eugene: Wipf & Stock, 2011.

Leaves, N. *Religion Under Attack: Getting Theology Right*. Salem: Polebridge Press, 2011.

Macnab, F. *Discover A New Faith. Energy For A Better Life*. Richmond: Spectrum Publications, 2011.

Miller, R. J. (ed) *The Future Of The Christian Tradition*. Santa Rosa: Polebridge Press, 2007.

Parkinson, L. *The World According To Jesus... His Blueprint For The Best Possible World*. Richmond: Spectrum Publications, 2011.

Sanguin, B. *The Advance Of Love. Reading The Bible With An Evolutionary Heart*. Vancouver: Evans & Sanguin Publishing, 2012.

Scott, B. B. *Trouble With Resurrection. From Paul To The Fourth Gospel.* Salem: Polebridge Press, 2010.

Stone, J. A. *Religious Naturalism. The Rebirth Of A Forgotten Alternative.* Albany: State University of New York Press, 2008.

Vosper, G. *Amen. What Prayer Can Mean In A World Beyond Belief.* Toronto: HarperCollins, 2012.

Webb, V. *Stepping Out With The Sacred. Human Attempts To Engage The Divine*. New York: Continuum International, 2010.

Wilson, B. *How Jesus Became Christian*. Canada: Random House, 2008

# About the Author

Rex A. E. Hunt, *PHF, MSc (Hons), GradDip(Communication Management)*

Rex Hunt is a retired minister of the Uniting Church in Australia, his last placement being at **The Church of St James, Canberra**, having served in parish settings in Victoria, Tasmania, NSW, and the ACT, spanning more than forty years.

In a previous life he was also the **National Director of Communications** with the National Assembly of the Uniting Church for nine years, and has done a short stint as **Acting Director**, School of Continuing Education at the NSW Synod's Centre for Ministry, in North Parramatta.

Along the way he was editor of *Ministry: A Journal of Continuing Education* (a Uniting Church professional development magazine) for 10 years, Founder and National co-ordinator of **The Network of Biblical Storytellers Australia/New Zealand** (1990-96), and Founding Director and Chair of the Management Team, **The Centre for Progressive Religious Thought, Canberra** (2002-09). He is now a Life Member of both organisations.

As part of his commitment to the progressive religion movement in Australia and New Zealand he is Chair of the Planning Team of **Common Dreams Conference of Religious Progressives**. Two Conferences have been held: **Common Dreams1 Conference**, with the theme "Progressive Religion as a Transforming Agent", in Sydney, NSW (2007) and **Common Dreams2 Conference**, with the theme "Living the 'progressive' Religion Dream", in Melbourne Vic. (2010). While **Common Dreams3 Conference** is planned for Canberra, ACT in September 2013 with the theme: "Midwives of Change: Progressives Shaping Religious Communities".

An Associate of the **Westar Institute** in Salem, Oregon, USA, he was for four years (2005-09) a member of its *Literacy & Liturgy Seminar*. In 2004 he was made a Paul Harris Fellow by **Rotary International** through the Rotary Club of Canberra Woden.

He and wife Dylis, live on the Central Coast of NSW (Australia). They have two married adult children and two grandchildren.